She is Limitless

The Power of Hope and Possibilities

Gifty Kwaku-Addison

She is Limitless

SHE IS LIMITLESS
The Power of Hope and Possibilities

Copyright © 2023 by Gifty K. Addison

All rights reserved. No portion of this publication without permission may be reproduced, stored in a retrieval system, or transmitted in any form or by any means – scanned, electronic, mechanical, photocopied or recorded without the author's written consent as it is strictly prohibited. Excerpts and links may be used, provided full and clear credit is given to the author with specific reference to the original content.

If you would like to use the author's book for short quotations or personal group study, this is permitted other than for review purposes. However, prior written permission must be obtained on request by emailing the author at gee@mumrevamped.co.uk.

ISBN Number Paperback: 978-1-7396607-6-5

Published by: Authentic Worth
Website: www.authenticworth.com
Email: info@authenticworth.com

She is Limitless

---- Dedication ----

I thank my Heavenly Father for His strength and wisdom in helping me to write and publish my second book.

There is HOPE for all mothers who are challenged, miserable, mentally and physically drained, burned out, overwhelmed and isolated but choose to dream.

Thanks to my beautiful family and my wonderful and supportive circle of friends who have become family!

She is Limitless

----- Contents Page -----

Introduction	1
Overview	4
Chapter 1 Accepting and Embracing your Extraordinary Life	9
Chapter 2 The Power of Mindset and Adopting a New Perspective	28
Chapter 3 Establishing Balance as a Mother to a Special Child	33
Chapter 4 Finding Meaning and Purpose in your Journey	37
Chapter 5 Change the Narrative and Dare to Dream	46
Chapter 6 Steps to Achieving your Dreams	53
Chapter 7 The Art of Delay	64
Chapter 8 Redefining What Success Means to You	70

She is Limitless

Chapter 9
Breaking Barriers: Shattering Limiting Beliefs — 84

Chapter 10 — 91
The Paralysis of Perfectionism

Chapter 11 — 98
Unmasking Imposter Syndrome

Chapter 12 — 103
Speaking Life and the Power of the Mind

Chapter 13 — 110
Recognising the Value of Self-Empowerment

Chapter 14 — 115
The Power of Wellness and Self-Care

Chapter 15 — 126
Self-Help and Coping Strategies

Chapter 16 — 137
Owning your Ideal Life

Epilogue — 142

References — 151

She is Limitless

---- Introduction ----

It can be difficult, but at the same time, rewarding to be a mother. The experience of becoming a mother is filled with love, happiness, sorrow, and heartache. However, this journey takes on a different meaning when you have loved ones who require ongoing care due to illness. Every mother of a child with special needs carries a tremendous burden. It comes with its unique set of challenges which can be overwhelming, but it also offers a life full of extraordinary, deeply fulfilling moments.

In these situations, balancing the constant demands of a household, a career or a business is challenging. In addition, being a good partner or spouse is exceptionally tough in these circumstances. Pursuing your passions while riding the rollercoaster of caring for special needs children turns into a long, laborious process that frequently results in burnout, sleepless nights, and being on auto-pilot.

When you are in these circumstances, it can be challenging to picture a future where you have the time, energy and resources to follow your dreams. However, pursuing your interests and aspirations are still possible regardless of your situation. The pressure of providing the best care for our loved ones becomes our life or part of our identity, but it doesn't have to be this way. We don't

She is Limitless

have to lose ourselves. Pursuing your passion is also necessary for personal growth and fulfilment.

She is Limitless helps special mothers recognise and step away from their current identity to look beyond their circumstances and discover their strengths whilst unlocking the hidden potential for a much healthier and fulfilled life. Writing this book was difficult as I had to deal with severe emotional issues while describing my parenting journey and the pitfalls I encountered.

You will be forced to consider important issues by defining the life you want and eliminating distractions that don't serve you. It provides readers with the guidance and motivation to make the most of what life has to offer and tap into their strengths and resilience for lasting change. You will learn how to use your challenges as sources of power and development to improve your life and the lives of your loved ones. As a result, you will be able to create a better future for yourself and your family when you have a newfound ambition and sense of power.

She is Limitless includes learning practical strategies for problem-solving, tackling stress and setting realistic goals to achieve significant milestones. By understanding various methods and techniques, you can regain the confidence to maximise the opportunities presented. With renewed hope, you can build an aspiring new life based on your values and beliefs. As you embark on the

She is Limitless

journey of self-discovery, you will find the strength to redefine yourself as a mother of a special needs child.

I can inspire, motivate and guide mothers in similar circumstances by highlighting my daily hardships.

She is Limitless assists readers in recognising their skills, shortcomings and the best ways to utilise them to accomplish their objectives. It includes problem-solving techniques, relaxation techniques and the value of building resilience. It discusses the challenges of coping with the guilt of attempting to create a life outside one's identity in order to break stereotypes and defy all preconceptions. These include overcoming self-limiting beliefs by being surrounded by like-minded people.

She is Limitless offers practical guidance on organising, succeeding and inspiring the reader to be expectant of the promises for the future with optimism and will discover how to harness problems as power sources for strength along the journey.

She is Limitless

---- Overview ----

I pictured myself growing up, getting married, having wonderful children, the ideal family and a successful career. I loved reading books about courageous women who constantly overcame adversity and achieved amazing outcomes. I aspired to be like them in contributing significantly to society. I soon discovered that my imagination was and still is my best quality.

Before sleeping at night, I daydreamed and envisioned myself in various occupations and settings. When I closed my eyes, I would visualise myself as a well-known author and successful entrepreneur. From a very early age, I wanted to write books which focused on empowering the young mind to dream.

My hopes and aspirations, however, were put on hold when I got pregnant at university and gave birth to my first daughter shortly before I turned 21. The 20s are often a period of exploration and self-discovery for young women, a time to figure out who they are, what they want to accomplish, follow their passions and find their place in the world.

After my education, I planned to travel to different parts of the world and experience different cultures, but I couldn't achieve this because of my unintended

She is Limitless

pregnancy in my 20s. I felt as though my entire world had ended. I was disappointed with myself and what people would think of me. Most of all, I felt there was no way I could work hard and achieve my dreams with a baby.

Raised in a Godly Christian home, this was a massive disappointment to my parents, who were both successful professionals and had high expectations of me. They worked tirelessly to provide the best opportunities in life. The social and cultural norms surrounding me were strong, and I felt increasingly ashamed. Although unhappy, they stood with me and supported me during my pregnancy.

My mother was especially devastated as she was the Chairperson of the Women's Fellowship in her church, and she felt the members would judge her. Many friends and family members gossiped that I became pregnant because I was a bad girl and rebellious. Even though I was careless and got pregnant early, I never stopped dreaming and wanted to prove the naysayers wrong.

"You are meant for greatness, Gifty!" My Daddy continuously told me. "So, you'll still succeed in whatever objectives you set for yourself." My parents always made a conscious effort to speak life and purpose into me and my brothers because they believed in the power of words and understood that what they said could influence the lives of their children and others around them.

She is Limitless

With this confidence booster, there was no 21st birthday party celebration. Instead, I was in the hospital preparing for the arrival of my baby. It was a rollercoaster of emotions, but I had the full support of my family and delivered a healthy baby girl in 1996. I returned to my education and worked extremely hard when my baby was old enough.

We were surrounded by doctors, lawyers, teachers, and other admirable role models in our social circles, and I was determined to please my parents. I had the drive to succeed to reach my full potential and win their approval, and I soon realised the secret to achieving my goals was to have hope and faith in my potential.

I realised that anything was possible if I was prepared to put in the work and never give up.

After having my baby girl, I kept the promise I made to my father that I'd return to university and complete my Law Degree, and I did so. My beautiful baby girl was the gift that kept me grounded; she was the wake-up call that aided me in gaining greater clarity, intense focus, and a feeling of direction. In her own way, she helped me develop a sense of self-belief and taught me that I, too, was destined for greatness.

She is Limitless

A few years after that, my second baby girl was born. Like her older sister, she was and still is beautiful and the most delightful precious being. I began to understand as time went on how much my parent's words had shaped my life. Their constant encouragement and positive affirmations gave me the confidence to pursue my dreams and overcome obstacles which came my way.

I often turned to my parent's teachings as I navigated life's ups and downs. I frequently referred to their advice in difficult situations. Finally, I understood their words had unfathomable power and used them to influence my life positively.

However, in 2008, my miracle Twin Angels, whom I call my "Dynamic Duo" came along, and my whole world came crumbling down. I would spend the rest of my life discussing special needs educational plans with physicians and therapists. My dreams and hopes were all shattered into fragments. I was heartbroken, and I felt as though my life was over. For a few years, I coasted along in a zombie-like state and threw myself into the caregiving role while attempting to hold down a career.

I was only concerned about getting through each day until I met a friend for lunch. He asked me a series of questions about the future of the girls. That's when I had to start dreaming again! Thirteen years after my Angels were born, as we lived in the Covid-era with schools,

She is Limitless

restaurants, pubs, and bars shut, and almost the whole world in partial/complete lockdown, I once again came to the shocking realisation that in my grief, I'd become complacent and stopped actively pursuing my dreams, taking life one day at a time and simply dealing with challenges as and when they arose.

What had become of the dreams and hopes for a better future for my children? A vow I had vehemently made to myself and, most importantly, their future. **The shock!** I knew I had to quit playing the victim and stop feeling sorry for myself. I had to stop playing mediocre if I wanted to leave a legacy for my children and others. Even as Caregivers, we dream about abundance, hope and creating the lifestyle we want. However, my decision to advance from a life of mediocrity to one of abundance was not easy. Over the years, I'd dealt with challenging issues leading to losing my self-esteem and confidence. The journey continues…

She is Limitless

---- Chapter 1 ----
~

Accepting And Embracing Your Extraordinary Life

"When you can't change the direction of the wind — adjust your sails."

H. Jackson Brown.

Receiving a diagnosis of a disability or additional needs for your child can be a tremendous shock for parents, along with an onset of worry for your loved one and your family's future. What should've been a beautiful day filled with joy and laughter for our family quickly became an evolving nightmare. There were no balloons or flowers, and my hopes and vision of friends and family welcoming our girls into the world were crushed.

As a child, I'd always dreamt of having beautiful, healthy children, and in an instant, that dream was taken away from me. The pain will never go away because the loss of my childhood dream was very significant at that moment. My feelings were all over the place. I went into the feelings of grief described below, though not in any exact order. Let's talk about:

She is Limitless

The Five Stages of Grief (An excerpt from my book; *My Journal with Twin Angels*):

1. Denial
Feeling numb is expected in the early days after bereavement. However, some people carry on as if nothing happened. Even if we know someone has died, believing they aren't coming back can be tough. It's also very common to feel the presence of someone who died as you faintly hear their voice or see them in dreams.

2. Anger
Anger is a natural emotion after someone dies. Death is cruel and unfair, especially when you feel someone died before their time and had plans together for the future. It's common to feel angry towards the person who died or feel remorseful for the tasks that weren't accomplished before their death.

3. Bargaining
When we're in pain, it's hard to accept we can't do anything to change it. Bargaining is when we start to make deals with ourselves and with God. We believe it will get better by acting in particular ways. It's common to find ourselves going over situations that happened in the past and asking the 'what if' questions, wanting to go back and change the circumstance in the hopes that it will turn out differently.

4. Depression

We often think of sadness and longing when dwelling on grief. This pain builds up intensely as it waves over many months or years. Life can feel like it no longer holds any meaning.

5. Acceptance

Grief comes in waves and feels like nothing will ever be right again. Gradually, most people find their pain easing, and it is possible to accept what happened. We won't always get over the death of our precious loved ones, but we can learn to live again while keeping the memories of those we've lost close to us.

These five stages, Denial, Anger, Bargaining, Depression and Acceptance, are often talked about as if they happen in the exact order, moving from one stage to the other, but this isn't usually the case. Fortunately, a few people who use the five stages of grief understand we all react to circumstances differently.

Kübler-Ross, in her writing, makes it clear that the stages are non-linear. People can experience these aspects of grief at different times and don't always happen in an orderly fashion. Depending on your challenges, you may not experience all the stages and may find that some stand out more than others.

She is Limitless

When my mum passed away, I had to be strong for the rest of the family. I don't recall breaking down, but grief hit me two years later, alone in my living room. I never realised until the day I didn't have the chance to grieve properly for my dear mother. That day brought back memories of promises I made to her about my goals for the future and working hard to ensure I left a lasting legacy.

In my state of hopelessness, I stumbled upon a quotation by Ellen Johnson Sirleaf that would transform my life forever: **"If your dreams don't scare you, they are not big enough!"** This short remark set off a chain reaction that brought back memories of my childhood self and aspirations. I then realised that fear was holding me back from working on myself and achieving my dreams, the fear of failure, judgement, and the unknown.

I had a lot of challenges to overcome, including self-doubt, prejudice, and juggling my personal and professional life. However, I was determined not to let obstacles define or get in my way. I continuously have big dreams and an unwavering determination to make them a reality. I quickly realised that change is essential to growth and success.

I became determined to embrace my journey and be open to discovering new opportunities and experiences. Throughout my journey, I found inspiration about the

She is Limitless

stories of other women who overcame adversity, and to date, they continue to achieve great accomplishments. These stories gave me courage to keep going when the road ahead seemed long and complex. They provided proof that I'm able to achieve anything if I put my mind to it and work hard to make it happen. I had to accept my fears into helping me achieve my objectives.

From Pain to Purpose: Transforming adversity into a life of meaning
A few years back, I became stranded in Atlanta en-route to San Francisco due to adverse weather conditions. While waiting at the terminal, I met a lady named Sally who introduced herself as a painter. She had a daughter with cerebral palsy, and we started discussing our families.

I was in awe after meeting this remarkable lady. Rather than allowing the difficulties to dampen her challenges, she uses her art as therapy and expression. Through her exhibitions and workshops, she showcases her talents and uses her paintings to capture the beauty and resilience of individuals with special needs worldwide. In addition, she uses her creativity to inspire others and embrace their dreams, regardless of obstacles. I was inspired!

I recently shared a photo of myself with one of my Angels on Instagram and later discovered the picture had been reshared on a specific page. I clicked the link to read more about them and saw images of stunning individuals and

She is Limitless

autistic children. As I read further, it revealed that Actress Holly Robinson Peete and her husband, Rodney Peete, a former NFL player, had founded an organisation. RJ, their son, is autistic.

The HollyRod Foundation is committed to educating the public and supporting families whose loved ones have been diagnosed with autism or Parkinson's disease. Celebrity mother of an autistic child, Holly Robinson Peete, uses her platform to promote autism inclusion and awareness. Many families facing similar difficulties have been motivated and empowered by her activities.

I've chosen to use my suffering as inspiration to write about my own experiences and make other mothers feel more empowered. Although I am not a well-known mother and have hardships as a result of my Twin Angels, I still believe in harnessing the power of writing to tell my story. The reason is simple: helping, connecting with others and giving back to the community to make a positive impact.

Life is unpredictable and can throw unexpected curveballs leaving us overwhelmed and helpless. Everyone experiences pain at some point in their lives. There are many distinct types of pain. But what if I told you that despair could also increase growth and positive change? Let's explore the concept of turning pain into purpose and how to use pain to create something meaningful.

She is Limitless

Life is full of hardships and challenges that leave us feeling lost and alone. Romans 5:1-5 (NIV) is a scripture that keeps me going, giving me peace and strengthening me through the various trials. I know suffering produces perseverance and shapes my character, giving me hope for a better tomorrow. What we do with pain shapes who we are. Some people allow the pain to consume them, while others make it a driving force to do something better or improve themselves. If you play the victim, you will always be seen as a victim.

"Hope does not put us to shame because God's love has been poured out into our hearts through the Holy Spirit." – Romans 5:5 (NIV).

What if we could channel our sufferings into something beneficial for our communities? Let's look at the following:

The meaning of pain
Before turning pain into purpose, we need to define and identify what we mean by pain. A painful feeling might be physical, emotional, or psychological. Several qualities can aggravate pain, such as trauma, disease, stress or loss. Pain can be acute or chronic, ranging from mild discomfort to severe agony.

Why turning pain into purpose is essential
Purpose is the reason we exist. It's what gives our lives meaning and direction. It's the driving force and motivation behind our decisions and actions. Turning pain into purpose can be a powerful way to transform your suffering into something positive. When we experience pain, it's easy to feel meaningless and a victim of our circumstances. However, we can find purpose in our lives by reframing our pain and view suffering as a chance to learn, grow and make a difference.

Steps to turn Pain into Purpose:

Acceptance is crucial
Acknowledging and accepting grief is the first step towards making it meaningful. Pain may appear physically, emotionally, or mentally. Therefore, it's critical to pinpoint the underlying source of suffering and deal with it head-on. To start, you have to admit your suffering and accept it. Through this process, you regain control of your emotions and stop letting them rule your life.

Determine the cause of your suffering
Finding the cause of sorrow is essential if you want to transform into purpose. Once you've acknowledged your pain, take some time to think about it. What is causing the pain? How does it make you feel? What impact has it had on your life? Is it a personal loss, a traumatic experience,

or something else? Once you identify the source of your pain, you can start working on ways to address it. Additionally, recognising and reflecting on pain can help you understand what you're going through.

Change your mentality
When facing adversity, having a pessimistic outlook on life is extremely easy. However, changing your perspective can help identify opportunities for growth and transformation arising from difficult situations. Instead of focusing on what you've lost or the pain you're going through, concentrate on what you'll gain from these experiences. Remember, every successful person has faced obstacles and setbacks, which are natural for the journey towards success.

Identify your purpose
Once you've found meaning in your pain, the next step is identifying your purpose. What do you intend to do about your pain? How can you use it constructively to create something positive? This could entail starting a support group for others who experience similar pain or taking on a more active role in a cause that's important to you.

Understand and learning from your pain
Each difficult situation has something to teach us. Instead of dwelling on the negative aspects of your pain, try to learn from it. What did you discover? How can you use this information to improve your life moving forward? The

She is Limitless

lessons you learn from pain can help you grow and develop personally.

Finding meaning in your pain
Finding purpose and meaning in your pain is the next step. Use your pain as fuel and put it to good use. This can be challenging but look for the lessons and opportunities your pain represents. For example, a traumatic breakup could teach about the significance of self-care or the value of healthy relationships. Finding meaning can help you overcome adversity and create a life filled with joy and fulfilment. You can also find meaning and purpose by identifying your values, passions and interests. This will help align your actions with goals to create a sense of purpose.

Utilise your pain to benefit others
One of the most significant ways to turn pain into purpose is by helping others who may be going through a similar experience. By sharing your story, you can encourage and uplift them. This can be through establishing a business, a blog, a support group, or volunteering your time to help others. Whatever you choose, make sure it aligns with your purpose and values. Helping others offers a sense of fulfilment and purpose whilst positively impacting those around you.

Concentrate on your goals
Setting defined goals is crucial to converting pain into meaning. What do you hope to accomplish? What kind of impact do you want to have on the world? Keep your eye on the objectives every day. A sense of purpose and direction will help you move forward and leave the pain behind.

It's more complex but turning suffering into purpose is possible. It takes patience, perseverance, consistency and determination. It may be a transforming journey which results in personal development, recovery, healing and fulfilment. It's challenging; however, finding meaning in your suffering can be a potent way to improve. We create a sense of purpose by embracing our pain and using it as a catalyst for change. Through this process, we overcome obstacles to inspire, encourage and enable others to follow our examples to make a difference in the world.

Remember, you're not alone in your pain; there is always hope for a better and brighter future, and your pain can be a source of strength and inspiration if you allow it to be. Your present situation should not determine your future. By accepting suffering and using it as a driving force for change, we develop a feeling of purpose. Through this process, we can overcome obstacles and enable others to be influenced by our attitudes and actions.

She is Limitless

There is always hope for a better future; if you let it, your suffering will be a learning curve, a source of strength and inspiration.

Embracing your unique journey is essential for several reasons:

Getting informed
Find out as much as you can about your loved one's condition and the resources available in the community to support them. As a result, you will feel more confident in your ability to care for your loved ones and better equipped to advocate for their needs.

Allowing yourself to grieve
It's acceptable to feel depressed or angry over your child's diagnosis. I still have those days where I feel sorry for myself and the curveballs I've had to deal with, even though some days are better than others. Please don't feel bad about going through this period because it's normal. Give yourself as much time as you can to grieve and analyse your feelings.

Unconditional self-acceptance
Many struggle to accept themselves as they are. The positive aspects are easier to accept, however, with all your talents, shortcomings and flaws, you embrace your special needs journey when you accept yourself for who you are. Allow yourself to experience all the emotions that

come with this path. Accepting yourself and the journey you're on will help to build self-esteem and confidence.

Resilience
By teaching how to deal with various obstacles, failures and how to develop coping mechanisms that work, embracing your special needs journey can assist in developing resilience.

Advocacy
Embracing your journey can help you stand up for yourself and other mothers facing similar situations. When you accept your unique challenges, you speak up for your beliefs and educate others about the various challenges, become an advocate and influence the voiceless.

Personal development
Embracing your special needs journey enables you to grow as a person. You could learn new skills, gain new insights and discover new passions that may not have been possible if you hadn't experienced the challenges you've encountered.

Relationship with others
Your journey can connect with others who share similar experiences. For example, consider joining a support group or making online connections through social media. It can be empowering to share your experiences with others. This can provide a sense of belonging and support,

She is Limitless

which is invaluable in navigating the challenges which come your way. Other emotions we experience as special needs mums include the following:

- Social exclusion
- Exhaustion – both physically and mentally
- Anxiety
- Feeling guilty and overwhelmed
- Financial stress
- Hopelessness

At the beginning of my journey, I bottled everything inside as my friends and family saw me as a strong woman. I didn't want to burden them with my struggles and felt no one understood what I was going through. As the years passed, I found myself sinking deeper into despair. I was frightened about the future of my girls, overwhelmed and filled with a sense of hopelessness I couldn't get rid of.

One day, as I listened to a podcast, I heard about journaling for the first time. Although it was initially challenging, since I wasn't used to putting my thoughts and feelings into words, I set aside time for journaling which became a crucial part of my life. I went online and purchased a lovely journal I enjoyed using. As I continued to write, I realised journaling is a potent tool for healing and self-discovery. It also helps me cope with the complex emotions and challenges of parenting my Twin Angels.

She is Limitless

I wrote about the challenges of caring for my girls, and as I continued to journal, I realised my perspective on life started to shift. I began to feel a sense of peace and clarity which I'd never experienced. I no longer felt demoralised as a victim of my circumstances, and journaling became a powerful tool for my growth. It was a way to release the pain and frustration I'd been carrying over the years.

If you are a special mum, think about using a journal. Your words heal yourself and others who may be going through similar difficulties. Journaling takes you to a place where you can be honest and release your vulnerabilities without worrying about judgment. You'll be surprised at how the power of writing can help confront fears and act as a catalyst to transform your pain into meaning.

Many special mums experience identity issues because they feel their role as a caregiver takes priority and overshadows their aspirations. As you struggle with all these unpleasant and painful emotions, know that:

You are enough
A significant part of my story, and one that most know or will get to know, is that my Twin Angels have been diagnosed with Autism and Epilepsy. They challenged what I viewed as perfect, worthy, meaningful, and valuable in life. I was broken; however, the treasures discovered aren't found in strength, performance, eloquence, character or confidence. Instead, they are in

She is Limitless

the broken places where beauty is found. It's God's love and compassion that's transformed my life up till now.

The ancient "Kintsugi" technique was discovered in the 15th century and is the art of putting broken pottery pieces back together with gold. Broken objects are repaired with natural gold powder to enhance and make them more beautiful, instead of trying to hide the scars.

This philosophy resonates with me as it represents an act of brokenness, resilience and healing. It's built on the ideology that by embracing our flaws and imperfections, we recreate ourselves to become more substantial and beautiful. Every broken part is unique, and instead of repairing the items fully, Kintsugi highlights scars as part of its unique design.

Cared for and honoured, a broken object assumes its past and becomes more resilient, beautiful, and precious. To find myself, I had to lose myself and endure the storms and challenging times to find healing and realise my full potential. Likewise, diamonds must undergo a rigorous process of extreme pressure and heat before becoming shiny and beautiful.

Having a child with a disability can be difficult. You wonder if anyone will ever understand what it's like to walk in your shoes. You're responsible for a child with special needs that makes you feel alone and invisible, but you are not.

She is Limitless

Remind yourself that you are enough and this means acknowledging who you are, complex and flawed with good and bad qualities. Set goals and pursue your passion in order to improve and elevate.

Affirmation Tips:

I am Beautiful
Your role as a special mum requires patience, love and dedication. Nonetheless, there are times when we go unnoticed as caregivers. Repeating the above to yourself builds great confidence and is a way to offer encouragement. This acknowledges your physical appearance, unique qualities, inner strength and resilience. This powerful affirmation brightens your day remembering you're loved and appreciated. You are beautiful, inside and out, doing a fantastic job, and you must constantly remind yourself of this.

I am Courageous
By affirming yourself as courageous, you recognise the sheer strength and determination it takes to navigate the rollercoaster of parenting a child with unique needs. Repeating this daily can help you feel more confident in your abilities as a mother to remind you that you aren't alone in your struggles. Caregiving is not an easy job; it's essential to acknowledge your difficulties and recognise your strength and bravery.

She is Limitless

I am Compassionate
Being a mum to a unique child is a role which requires a great deal of empathy, compassion, patience and understanding. You display compassion if you put in the work, time, effort, and love necessary to care for your child. Remember to be kind to yourself and recognise the strength and resilience it takes to navigate this role.

I am Brave
It takes courage to face challenges and the uncertainties of raising a child with additional needs. Yet, you consistently rise to the occasion to care for your child in the best way possible. Know that you are brave and strong, and your unwavering dedication to your child and family is a testament to your bravery. Your efforts are making a difference in your child's life and the lives of those around you. Be proud of what you do as you continue to press on.

I am Gracious
The challenges of raising a unique child require grace, and you should be proud of yourself for the love and care provided to your child. Your willingness to take on this role to support your child shows you are compassionate and gracious. Your dedication to your child is admirable, and you should always be celebrated.

She is Limitless

I am Admirable
Your role is challenging and requires exceptional strength to navigate this journey. However, your commitment to providing the best possible care is one of true inspiration. Your tenacity and resilience in adversity make you a noble and remarkable mother. It's essential to recognise your admirable qualities and take pride in the hard work you do every day.

I am Resilient
Navigating the daily obstacles takes an immense amount of courage and determination. Yet, you show resilience daily by advocating for your child's needs and seeking additional resources. As a mother reading this book, I am sure you have endured many setbacks. However, you have persevered through them all. Your intense devotion and dedication to your child's well-being are a testament to your strength, unwavering commitment and resilience. You continue to show up each day for your child and your family.

The above are qualities displayed as a mother nurtures and protects their loved ones, which will never go unnoticed. They appreciate it more than you'll ever know. Be proud of who you are and the unique child you're parenting because they bring so much joy and delight with each passing day.

---- Chapter 2 ----
~

The Power of Mindset and Adopting a New Perspective

"Once you choose hope, anything is possible."

Christopher Reeve.

Your mindset is a powerful tool in your journey as a special mum, enabling you to work hard and achieve your dreams. This is because your mindset shapes how you think, perceive and respond to challenges, setbacks and opportunities. As a result, you can overcome obstacles and accomplish your goals by developing a growth mindset and focusing on possibilities instead of limitations.

Moving away from the miserable life I'd created for myself and my loved ones wasn't easy. There were many tears, and I prayed daily for God to show me what He wanted me to do. I always enjoy supporting women and am passionate about educating the *"Girl Child"* and organising charitable events to raise funds towards worthy causes.

She is Limitless

As time passed, I began helping women from all walks of life get back into work after taking a career break or staying at home looking after their unique children. I assisted them with their CV's and how to improve their interview techniques as they had been out of the workforce for so long. When I shared my story with the women I came into contact with, I saw its impact on them. I've since started a blog documenting my journey and connecting with other women and special needs mothers striving towards their dreams.

Helping others gives me a sense of fulfilment and joy.

Deciding to live on my terms rather than what others expected of me gave me the freedom to make healthy choices. It also meant being true to myself. To live life on your terms, you must define what that means. Let's take a look at the following points:

- What is your belief system?
- What are your values?
- What are your goals?
- What are your priorities?

Adopting a new perspective is a powerful way for a special mum to live a more purpose-filled life. It's about being

She is Limitless

intentional with your choices to help find greater meaning and fulfilment in your role and professional endeavours. Once you understand this, you can start to align your life with your vision. Writing and documenting a book about *My Journey with Twin Angels* highlights the power of possibility and the quote from Napoleon Hill which says: "Whatever the mind conceives, it can achieve."

Through my blog, I've reached out to other mothers and helped them change their perspectives to have a positive outlook on life. Let's look at the following tips to consider:

Tips:

Discover how to dance around your fears
Worrying about your child's future and well-being as a special parent is normal. Life might be stressful, but you must learn to dance with your fears instead of letting them restrict you. This enables you to step out of your comfort zone and have a more fulfilling life.

Focus on the here and now
Getting caught up worrying about the future or dwelling on the past is distracting. Worrying doesn't resolve our problems or make them go away. Instead, learn how to spend quality time with your family and loved ones, focus on living life fully and find joy in the small moments which make you happy.

She is Limitless

Accept your imperfections
As a special mum, it's easy to feel you aren't doing enough. Instead, embrace your flaws and always do your best with what you have. Making mistakes and doing your best in highly challenging situations is okay. That's how you learn to blossom.

Practice self-compassion
I used to second-guess whether I was doing all the right tasks for my Angels, providing them with the best care possible, which only made me mentally ill. Being kind to yourself is crucial, especially when facing difficulties and challenges. Practice self-compassion by speaking to yourself with kindness and understanding. Show yourself the same level of love, care and compassion you would show your loved ones and close friends.

Find new meaning in your caregiving role
I've decided to use my writing skills to encourage mothers in a similar situation. Instead of getting frustrated with your child's diagnosis and feeling sorry for yourself, take time out and have a break. Reflect on how being a special needs mum has brought meaning and purpose to your life. This may include your deep connection with your child, the lessons learnt about resilience and strength, or the impact you've had in the lives of others. You can join support groups, volunteer your time or learn a skill. Whatever you choose to do, find people with a positive outlook who will inspire you to follow your passion.

She is Limitless

Keep it real

Though it may be challenging occasionally, don't compare yourself or your child to another person. Learn to put more emphasis on improvement and progress than perfection. Setting reasonable expectations for yourself and your loved one is crucial. You are very capable of handling moments independently, and other times, asking for assistance when needed. I wasn't the type of person who'd ask for help and was always exhausted. Now, I know it's good to take a break when necessary and seek out guidance when relevant.

---- Chapter 3 ----
~

Establishing Balance as a Mother to a Special Child

"Once you accept that your child will be different, not better or worse; just different, that is the first step."

Unknown.

As a mum of four girls and of differing ages, it would be easy to see why I am so busy. It takes a lot of work to keep track of their schedules alongside my full-time job and supported living business. It's a daily struggle to balance it when the youngest two are Angels with additional needs, adding a lot of extra appointments to our lives. Finding balance as a special needs mum is essential to avoid caregiver burnout. I had to be disciplined if I wanted to accomplish my goals.

As a mother to my Twin Angels, we hardly follow a schedule at home as it's practically impossible. We go through some days where the girls are asleep by 8.00 pm. However, there are certain nights when one or both get very little sleep or none. As a result, I am always exhausted and have fewer energy reserves which impacts my day and my jobs. I had to promise that I'd squeeze in a couple of hours each day whenever the girls let me have some free time. This would often occur at the end of the workday. I said to myself that it had to be done, and so I did. In doing so, I also established a routine where I could have some me-time that didn't require a set structure. Depending on how my day was going, it would involve:

- Going for a walk to get some fresh air
- Having a relaxing bath and reading a book
- Locking myself in a quiet space to recharge my mind, body and soul

The secret to balance is being in tune with yourself and your family members. Some weeks are chaotic at home when illness, additional appointments, and work schedules are added to the mix. Finding some structure in your routine while remaining adaptable and flexible is the key. This helps to create a sense of predictability, with enough time set aside for other activities. Let's take a look at the following tips:

Tips:

Put self-care first
Even if it only takes a few minutes each day to pray, meditate, work out, or read a book, taking care of yourself is essential as it replenishes your energy. Recharging your batteries is necessary since you can't pour from an empty cup.

She is Limitless

Join a supportive network
Connecting with other parents of special needs children can be beneficial. You can do this by joining support groups or online communities. These groups can provide understanding, support, and validation, as well as offer practical advice and resources. If there is none locally, consider starting one yourself.

Simplify your schedule
I am proud of my propensity for multitasking. However, I quickly realised that I also needed help in completing my jobs. I eventually became what you may call a "Jack of all trades, master of none!" You must understand that you can't do everything at once. Instead, simplify your schedule as much as possible by delegating, prioritising what is truly important and letting go of the rest. Approaching tasks this way will help you regulate stress levels better and avoid burnout.

Seek professional help
Some cultures disregard people getting help, so most tend to suffer in silence. I had to seek help when I hit the depths of despair and couldn't see a way out. I avoided talking to anyone about it since I had to do this for myself. Taking the first step towards getting the support you need is vital through seeking professional assistance if you feel overwhelmed, overburdened, or your child's needs require more support than you can provide. Therapy, counselling, or working with a special needs educator or

therapist are all examples of support. You can contact a local therapy centre or use trusted online resources to get support.

Adopt a positive attitude
While caring for a special needs child can be challenging, embracing the positives is crucial. Celebrate your child's strengths, talents and accomplishments and focus on the joy and love of being a mother. My attitude and daily feelings impact my thoughts, energy levels, and actions. Being optimistic doesn't mean we ought to pretend everything is going well when dealing with difficulties. No, far from that, but you must try to remain positive to avoid becoming a victim or an enslaved person to your circumstances.

Finding balance as a mother to a special needs child requires addressing and releasing negative thoughts and emotions. As much as we detest failure, it occasionally happens. These are the periods you discover more about yourself. However, we mustn't dismiss these feelings to learning and growing from them. After reaching my breaking point, I could no longer push myself to pursue any of the goals I had set for myself. I lacked energy, and procrastination became the norm. My confidence was affected, and so did my career. Eventually, I neglected my well-being and stopped exercising, writing and doing all the things I once loved to do.

---- Chapter 4 ----
~

Finding Meaning and Purpose in your Journey

"Remember that wherever your heart is, there you will find your treasure."

Paulo Coelho.

Autism, epilepsy, and all the other illnesses were not the grand plans I had for my twin pregnancy. However, I understand that I don't have to compromise. I've learnt that everything is possible as long as I have faith and belief. As a strong and beautiful mother navigating the world of special needs, you, too, can change your story! Being a carer can be taxing and stressful, but it can also be rewarding and filled with love.

Remember; you don't have to redefine yourself entirely because you are the mother of a unique child.

This journey is an opportunity for development, education and transformation. One strategy which worked for me

She is Limitless

was constantly reminding myself that raising my Twin Angels is a privilege, not just a responsibility. It's an incredible and humbling privilege. I was a young girl; now, I am a woman with responsibilities, interests, dreams and aspirations. Thinking this way enables me to focus on personal growth and development. I had to change my viewpoint and look for ways to positively influence my family and the lives of those around me rather than seeing my Twin Angels as burdens.

Finding opportunities to give back to the community can also be part of living a life with purpose and, for example, creating the time to volunteer your services or resources to support an organisation with special needs families or advocates for disability rights. I do this for my secondary school by organising charitable events and raising funds to assist the "Girl Child". By giving yourself away through helping and devoting your time to others, you will find fulfilment and meaning outside your role as a Carer.

Another way to change the narrative is to share your story with others. We have no idea what other people are going through, and by speaking openly and honestly about our struggles, we can educate and inspire others going through similar challenges. As I began sharing my story, many women started to contact me. I was astonished to learn that not all of them had children with additional needs, whilst other women had no children, but my story resonated and gave them the determination to keep

She is Limitless

fighting. Additionally, you can work to dispel myths and prejudices about parenting children with special needs by using your voice to make a difference!

You never know the lives you'll touch or how much of an impact it will be to share your story.

When I was younger, I fell in love with a song called "Never Give Up" by Yolanda Adams. I'd play the song repeatedly whilst soaking up the lyrics. Some parts of the song have remained with me and will continue for the rest of my life. It reads:

"To fulfil your divine purpose
You've gotta answer when you are called
So don't be afraid to face the world
Against all odds
Keep the dream alive; don't let it die; if something deep inside
It keeps inspiring you to try, don't stop
And never give up; don't ever give up on you
Don't give up!"

I had many dreams as a child and still have them today. Through Yolanda Adam's song and other experiences, I am constantly learning about perseverance and not giving up on creating a better future for myself and others. The

She is Limitless

results won't fall in my lap or happen overnight; I have to be willing to work for it against all odds.

If you search deeply within yourself, you'll discover and be proud of the unique qualities that make you who you are. Although focusing on caring for a child with additional needs can be challenging, taking a break and considering the bigger picture is vital. This means taking time out to consider how you want your future to look like and making gradual but consistent efforts to reach your objectives.

By doing this, you'll manage your stress levels better and have the strength and clarity to be the best mother you can be for your children. You'll be motivated to work towards your objectives. Additionally, ensuring that those closest to you are considerate, kind, understanding and empathetic is essential and can offer ongoing support.

Build your village, or what I refer to as my "Circle of Support."

The right people around you will understand how you feel; you shouldn't feel guilty about asking for assistance from them. You are in control of your identity, regardless of your circumstances. Keep sight of your strength and the capacity to overcome life's challenges and hold fast to the hope you have. No matter your difficulties, never let being the mother of a child with special needs define who you are. You are strong and more capable than you realise. You can overcome any obstacle when you believe in yourself and have confidence in your skills and abilities. There will be difficult days, but remember there is always hope, and you'll not walk this path alone.

Remember that life guarantees nothing, and anything can happen at any time. Therefore, maintaining flexibility and being open to new possibilities is crucial since they frequently result in new experiences and opportunities. Finally, be proud of all you've achieved. You are more than just a carer! Don't let anyone tell you otherwise. Above all else, remember to be who you are. Your identity is built on strengths, aptitude, and bravery. Find your village and be encouraged to know that you'll never be alone on your journey to overcome obstacles. Let's look at the following tips to help encourage you throughout the journey:

Tips:

Surround yourself with positive people
Your well-being and mental health are significantly impacted by the people you surround yourself with. A positive circle of support can provide emotional encouragement, practical help and understanding. When you feel disheartened or overwhelmed, they give you a new perspective, helpful counsel, and reassurance.

She is Limitless

Finding people who relate and understand your position is crucial, whether or not they're special needs parents. Spend time with those who are positive when you're feeling down. Positive people can inspire and motivate you as they remain optimistic and look for the positives in the most challenging circumstances. Establishing healthy boundaries and avoiding people who bring negativity into your life is something to be aware of before it escalates.

You'll feel better when you build meaningful and long-lasting, important relationships. Surrounding yourself with positive people boosts confidence and helps to overcome challenges. Instead, they help shift your focus and stay motivated. Spending more time with people who enrich your life is more beneficial as you'll start embracing their thinking methods.

Get rid of the *Special Needs Mum Tag!'*
Though stigmas and societal expectations are associated with the designation "Special Needs Mum," remember, you are more than a label. My Twin Angels are a big part of my life, but they don't entirely define me. Despite how difficult it is, I am a unique individual with interests, skills and passions, and I am proud of my caregiving role. I want to share the following points as a source of encouragement to keep you going:

- Focus on other obligations in life, such as your profession, hobbies, and interests and embrace your

She is Limitless

individuality – make time and pursue what you enjoy doing
- Connect with people and groups who share similar experiences and goals – you can build new friendships and expand your social circle beyond the special needs community
- Cherish the times throughout the day that make you happy
- Plan self-care activities into your schedule to maintain a healthy balance
- Schedule socialising and enjoyable activities with friends and family
- Work on your personal development and growth
- Pursue goals, dreams, and aspirations aside from parenting
- Look for new experiences that bring you happiness
- Stop and relax when necessary!
- Think about the rewarding facets of parenting, not only raising children with special needs
- Find a mentor or support group that provides compassion, understanding and encouragement
- Spend time with loved ones and friends who understand your circumstances
- Engage in leisure and gratification-promoting activities
- Focus on the positives of parenting special needs children

She is Limitless

- To maintain your identity and worth, take some time out for yourself
- Develop the ability to be adaptable to changes in your parenting circumstances
- Appreciate the moments when tasks/projects run smoothly

Remember the small victories and progress you make in your parenting journey. Acknowledge the challenges and the triumphs faced, and you will see how those challenges can be overcome through being resilient and having a positive mindset each day.

Creating a positive identity
Your life should reflect an optimistic outlook when you do what is right. Positivity motivates us to take action towards our objectives, whilst pessimism makes us less motivated. Although it might be challenging, developing a positive identity as a mother of children with special needs isn't impossible. To get started in creating a positive identity, apply the following steps:

- Focus on developing deeper relationships with your children – be careful to talk with them in honesty and have quality time with them
- Join community groups with mothers who're going through the same circumstances as you – this serves as a great support system to learn about yourself and others in similar situations

She is Limitless

- Make yourself a top priority – Remember to take care of yourself and engage in activities that make you happy

- Ask for help from an expert when you need it – speak with a therapist who can give objective advice which can be beneficial to your mental and emotional well-being

- Ask your family and other friends for help or guidance – you'll need a strong support network to guide you through this new stage of life

- Take a step back and concentrate on the good things in life – endeavour to find delight in the day-to-day interactions with your children and cherish every special moment with them

- Find ways to communicate who you are and what you believe in – for example, developing a new activity, devoting time to writing, being creative by making artwork or participating in your local neighbourhood

- Finally, be patient with yourself – it's acceptable when adjusting to a new role as it will take some time. Eventually, you'll find your way and create a positive sense of self.

---- Chapter 5 ----
~

Change the Narrative and Dare to Dream

"When you reach an obstacle, turn it into an opportunity. You have the choice. You can overcome and be a winner, or you can allow it to overcome you and be a loser. The choice is yours and yours alone. Refuse to throw in the towel. Go that extra mile that failures refuse to travel. It is far better to be exhausted from success than to be rested from failure."

Mary Kay Ash.

Life as a mother of special needs children can be challenging and unpredictable, yet you should never give up on your dreams and aspirations. Getting bogged down in the day-to-day responsibilities of caring for your loved one can be overwhelming. However, it's important to remember that you have the power to dream big and set goals for yourself. Take some time to ponder on what you want to achieve and the steps you'll take to make those aspirations a reality.

She is Limitless

As a special mum, you can use the opportunity to embark on an entrepreneurial journey which can be both exciting and challenging. As I work in a demanding field and am still deciding what the future holds for my Twin Angels, I decided to launch a side business. I may consider quitting my job in the corporate world to devote myself to taking care of them. Who knows? When that time comes, I will have peace of mind and not worry about how we will cope financially.

You will also possess unique insights and experiences which are valuable in creating a business that serves others. You can get started by figuring out your objectives and ambitions. Once this has been established, reflect on important questions and address the following:

- What do you want to achieve?
- What are your passions and interests?

Write them down and keep them close as a reminder of what you are working towards. Finally, consider how your unique skills and interests can translate into a viable business. I started doing this by creating a vision board, a valuable tool for helping define concrete objectives. Next, break down your goals into smaller, manageable and achievable steps. Doing this makes your tasks less daunting and makes the vision more attainable. After this, carry out one action at a time and celebrate each

She is Limitless

accomplishment. Remember that starting and being consistent is crucial no matter how slow the results are. Dream big and figure out how to turn your aspirations into a reality because you deserve happiness, peace, and fulfilment. Be resourceful and make the most of the talents and abilities you acquire whilst caring for your children with special needs.

Dream about solutions to your problems; search for new sources of information and consider what you can accomplish with the resources obtained. After that, take a moment to reflect on your progress and identify areas for improvement. Finally, keep an eye on your goals, and develop a plan. Consult with trustworthy friends and family members to seek communities to support your goals.

Mentors aid your progress by offering guidance and suggestions.

Remember to have reasonable expectations and be open to making mistakes when pursuing your objectives, as this is how you learn faster. As you advance, keep telling yourself that you deserve a fulfilling life and that you are enough. Your bravery and tenacity lay the groundwork for your success and the assurance you need to move forward. Use the abilities gained from raising your

She is Limitless

children with special needs and allow yourself to be motivated by the methods employed to assist them. Experiment, take chances and try something new. You are uniquely positioned to change the world as the mother of a child with special needs.

Actively seek out channels or explore avenues to speak up and act to bring about significant change in your community. Find methods to inspire others, motivate people, share your stories, and encourage other mothers experiencing similar challenges. No matter what challenges life presents, demonstrate to the world that nothing is impossible.

Remember to relish the journey, the triumphs and joys. Never lose hope, doubt or question your abilities, and refuse to let anyone tell you your dreams are unattainable. Remember that anything is possible when you have faith and tenacity. Honour your dreams daily; don't allow fear to hold you back. Life is an adventure; be open to the journey and see what the world has to offer.

"Dare to dream; dare to do" goes the Proverb.

You can fulfil all your ambitions with perseverance, dedication, and determination. Although it can be difficult, living a life with meaning is possible. Your

She is Limitless

objectives, dreams, and abilities, not your child's impairment, should define you. It can be challenging to juggle the obligations of parenting a unique child, but making time for yourself and your aspirations is vital. Remember to care for your needs, feed your spirit, and believe in the power of your dreams. With the knowledge and experience acquired through raising your special children, you are uniquely positioned to enhance the future of your family and, ultimately, others around you.

How to handle the guilt of daring to dream
I understand this can be not easy, as you may feel your focus should solely be on your child's needs. However, it's natural to have aspirations, just like every other parent. Professional counselling or support groups are recommended to help you work through these emotions. However, it's critical to recognise that pursuing other interests and being an extraordinary mother is acceptable.

I was miserable when I devoted myself to being a full-time caregiver as I was wallowing in self-pity and operating in mediocrity. Taking care of yourself and finding ways to relax and unwind will help to manage the emotions connected to adjusting. Think about speaking to other parents that go through similar experiences. They can enlighten and reassure you that having different interests aside from raising children is possible.

She is Limitless

Speaking with a qualified mental health expert can help you learn more about handling the emotions of being a mother with a special needs child, finding your identity, and daring to dream again. There are helpful resources on the internet which offer direction and insight including blogs, webinars and support groups.

Do not compare yourself to others; remember that your dreams are as significant as everyone else's.

It's easy to feel inferior that you don't measure up to other parents, especially those who don't have the same challenges as you do. We're all on a unique journey, so comparing yourself to others is unproductive. Daring to dream is simply recognising your needs and taking action to pursue your goals alongside your role as a caregiver. Let's look at some of the tips on the ways you can take action to pursue your goals:

Tips:

Identify your passion and interests
What are you passionate about? What are your hobbies and interests? Spend some time thinking about moments that make you happy.

She is Limitless

Set achievable goals
Start by setting small achievable goals which align with your passions and interests. Eventually, you can gradually create bigger, more ambitious goals as you accomplish them step-by-step.

Be adaptable
Your life can be unpredictable, so prepare to be flexible and adjust your plans when necessary.

Believe in yourself
Remember that you are a powerful and resilient woman. With the right mindset and supportive environment, you are capable of dreaming big and achieving your goals. You will overcome any obstacles that come your way when you take the time to self-reflect.

Never give up
Pursuing your dreams isn't always simple, but stay determined and don't give up. Keep moving forwards even when progress is slow. Consistency is key! Don't use lack of time as an excuse. If you can't prioritise your purpose, it's not that important to you. On the other hand, if finding and fulfilling your purpose is of high priority, you'll make time for it.

---- Chapter 6 ----
~

Steps to Achieving Your Dreams

"The only limit to the height of your achievements is the reach of your dreams and your willingness to work for them."

Michelle Obama.

Whilst achieving your goals can be difficult, it's attainable with the appropriate Attitude, Plans and Actions (A.P.A).

Define your purpose
Your purpose is evident as an extraordinary mother and deeply meaningful. In the times and seasons we're in, it's essential to look within ourselves to discover what our purpose is.

Take some time to consider what gives your life meaning.

She is Limitless

Your life's purpose is your mission statement which will help to make your mark in the world. Be prepared to dig deeper to discover hidden abilities to obtain meaningful answers. Once you pinpoint this, you'll have a renewed sense of direction. You can change careers, start a business and have a better work/life integration. Whatever your goals, it often takes a minor adjustment to shift your perspective.

What is my purpose in life?
I've asked myself this question numerous times in past years. To take ownership of my life, I had to quit playing the victim and refuse to let my circumstances define me. I also prayed for God to grant me direction and clarity towards my vision. Whilst I may not always feel that it was the right season or the best thing to do, my mission is now clear, and I've decided to turn my pain into purpose and my mess into a message for all mothers struggling to make meaning of their lives.

Remain true to yourself and don't live your life according to other people's expectations. We can never find or understand our purpose by seeking external validation. It's okay if you don't know what your life's purpose is right now. However, one of the most significant errors we tend to make is failing to search for our purpose. For this reason, what brings you joy in the process of finding your purpose? I would suggest taking the following points into account:

She is Limitless

What change would you like to see in the community and the world?
Your purpose in life isn't static and can evolve over time. As a result, be open to new experiences, learn from your mistakes and keep growing and evolving. Be the change you wish to see within the community.

Determine your why
To determine your WHY, spend time reflecting on what motivates you. Be clear about what you want to achieve. Starting with PURPOSE can help to establish your WHY. My WHY is being able to provide for my family and leave a legacy behind for them and others around me. Everyone has a WHY, a deep-seated purpose that drives and inspires us. Your WHY is what you believe in, which will encourage you to dream bigger. Once you understand your why, you can articulate what makes you feel fulfilled and what drives your behaviour when you're at your best, you can live every day by taking action towards your goals.

Set achievable goals
I came across the term "Goal Digger", which seemed funny to me then, as I'd only heard of "Gold Digger." I was tempted to think it was a typo error, but upon reflection and further reading, Goal Digger means that an individual is ambitious and extremely clear about what they want to achieve. The label: "Gold Digger" describes someone who uses others for opportunities and financial gain. In contrast, Goal Diggers have dreams, goals and aspirations

for independence, a success-based mindset and their version of happiness. Simply put, a Goal Digger never stops digging and working towards their goals.

Take baby-steps towards your goals
Spend time envisioning what success looks like, as you will find inspiration and motivation from this. Your goals can be accomplished by breaking them down into manageable, sequential steps. Making progress towards your goals will give you a true sense of fulfilment.

Write down your goals and make sure they are specific, measurable, achievable, relevant, and time-bound, also known as the SMART acronym. We feel a sense of accomplishment when we achieve our goals, such as purchasing a new home or launching a business. Having a clear mission and purpose takes these goals to a higher level. Let's discuss your SMART goals below and fill out what they are:

Specific:
_____
_____
_____
_____
_____
_____

She is Limitless

Measurable:
_____
_____
_____
_____
_____
_____
_____

Achievable:
_____
_____
_____
_____
_____
_____
_____

Relevant:
_____
_____
_____
_____
_____

She is Limitless

_____
_____

Time-Bound: _____
_____
_____
_____
_____
_____
_____

Create a plan of action for achieving your dreams and follow it. Determine the resources, tools and skills required to reach your objectives and break them into manageable chunks while setting deadlines for each task. This will help you stay on track. Writing out your goals can make you focus on what's important.

Take action
We have big dreams and goals but often must remember that taking action will bring them to fruition. Start with small steps and build momentum as you progress. Be consistent in your efforts and be willing to learn from your experiences and modify your strategy wherever necessary. Ask for feedback from others and use it to improve your techniques. Once you start making minor

She is Limitless

improvements and alterations to the habits developed over time, it eventually produces tremendous results.

How can you make your actions easier?

What are the small tasks you need to do every day?

How can you create a conducive environment to take action?

Write them below:

_____
_____
_____
_____
_____
_____
_____
_____
_____
_____

She is Limitless

Stay motivated
You want to achieve your dreams by reminding yourself of your "Why" and the reasons behind it. My Twin Angel's resilience, eyes, smiles, and touch gives me strength and hope to keep moving.

What motivates you to carry on?
Work on your goals, celebrate your victories and maintain a positive attitude in the face of adversity.

Look for resources
Explore more resources or request for help to achieve your goals.

Step outside your comfort zone
It took a lot of courage and sleepless nights to step out and share my story with the world. I've had to make minor adjustments, such as setting aside time to work on my goals. Change happens when we challenge ourselves to step out of our comfort zone. Doing so opens us to new knowledge, opportunities and experiences. By doing this, I am setting an example for my older girls and others facing similar challenges.

Track your progress
Stay inspired by recording your progress and checking them frequently.

She is Limitless

Understanding and learning from failures
Failure is a necessary component of learning. Therefore, when you fail, you learn from the experiences as a chance to progress.

Celebrate your achievements
Celebrating your achievements is vital, no matter how small they are. Recognising your accomplishments boosts self-esteem and self-confidence, which encourages the attitude of working hard, staying motivated and remaining committed to achieving our dreams.

Look for mentors
Choose a mentor you believe has a positive impact on you and make the most of their shared experiences. Remember that perseverance and diligence are the secrets of success. Do not give up!

Remain focused and disciplined
It may be difficult for a special mum to balance the demands of her caregiving responsibilities alongside her aspirations. However, with determination and consistency, we remain focused on our goals and stay committed as devoted mothers. We must take action and create the life we want to ensure everything happens according to plan.

I maintain discipline by scheduling my time efficiently and completing fewer tasks first to prevent burnout. I also start my day early to plan my written blogs. Staying focused on my goals and avoiding distractions prevents me from slowing down. It's important to remain disciplined regardless of how you feel about your actions and routines and prioritise your dreams. You can do the essential tasks as long as you maintain your discipline.

Maintain your optimism and believe in yourself
It would help if you didn't give up when things are difficult. Remember that achieving your dreams is a journey which requires time and effort until you get to your destination. Your standards are elevated when you surround yourself with people who make you happy and have the drive and tenacity to share your ambitions. Once you believe this, you will be unstoppable.

Grow your mindset
To foster a growth mindset is similar to going on a treasure hunt. It's the opportunity to keep discovering new ways of growth that help us find more fulfilment in life. A growth mindset is a firm conviction that your abilities and talents can be developed and improved through hard work and perseverance. Let's look at the following activities:

Do you have a clear idea of your vision?

Do you have a clear idea of your goals?

What steps have you put into practice to achieve them?

She is Limitless

Write them down below:

--- Chapter 7 ----
~

The Art of Delay

Procrastination prevents you from achieving your objectives and ambitions. Such behaviour is challenging to break; however, this habit must be dealt with if you want your dreams to become a reality and your goals manifested. About six weeks into the Covid lockdown, my workplace responded early to the crisis and asked employees to work from home. This was extremely impressive as other companies took longer to respond to the global pandemic.

However, I struggled to work from home for the first two weeks as I missed the constant buzz in the office, having lunches and quick catchups with friends and work colleagues. In addition, I suffered constant headaches from using a laptop and trying to navigate through what were many pages of research. This was highly stressful until I purchased a second screen and set up Home Office in my spare bedroom.

I created a workspace which allowed me to prioritise tasks and work more efficiently, and at first, I was elated at this new way of working. I was saving money on parking and

She is Limitless

travel costs and would no longer wake up at 5.00 am to get ready for work when my household was fast asleep. Right? Wrong! I found myself lying awake through some nights, mind racing, and on those nights when I managed to fall asleep, I would wake up before 5.00 am. I hear you ask – why?

With my newly found extra time, this was a question I kept asking myself, and then one day, BAM! I had a lightbulb moment – PROCRASTINATION! That was it! I was putting off tasks until a later date. It suddenly dawned on me that I was one of those individuals who had 1,001 tasks pending. Tasks I should've completed were still pending; many of the deadlines I'd set for myself had been missed.

Those who've read my first book, My Journey with Twin Angels, would know about my struggles with them. I wanted set up multiple businesses and share my story with the world to inspire other mothers. However, all I had to show were half-written pages of journals and blogs on my Journey with my Angels. What's been my reason for not completing these tasks? What happened to my vows to create a better future for my children? Where was the evidence I was planning towards such a future? The answer always came relatively easy to me…

Time!
Really? And now, suddenly, I had enough time on my hands. What exactly was I doing with my time? I could no

She is Limitless

longer use lack of time as an excuse not to complete my tasks. I've been given time to sit, think, plan and act accordingly, so no more excuses!

Chronic procrastinators may exhibit some of the following habits:

- Putting tasks off until the last minute to when they've had plenty of time to complete it
- Procrastinators may have trouble managing their time effectively, which results in a backlog of tasks that need to be finished
- Putting off difficult chores for an extended period of time
- Getting distracted by non-essential activities such as social media and other forms of entertainment when their time should be spent on more meaningful projects
- Procrastinators underestimate how long tasks take, eventually putting them off until much later and being overwhelmed, stressed, and, unfortunately, produce hurried work.
- They avoid taking responsibility for their actions, refuse to remain accountable and are more likely to blame others or external circumstances for their procrastination.

Does any of the above sound like you? Do you ever find yourself procrastinating? Of course, but have you thought

She is Limitless

about the actual cost of procrastination? Procrastination, as the saying goes, is the thief of TIME – To procrastinate is to delay and put off completing a task. Procrastinating is deferring tasks as it wastes time and ends in nothing being done. The proverb is a quotation from the poem; Night Thoughts by Edward Young.

For the reasons below, procrastination will always be the thief of time because:

- Time never stops, never slows down and always moves
- Once it's gone, it's gone!
- Time is the one resource that can never be replaced

For the first time, I began to think about this saying in the context of my life on earth. I'd accepted and believed that God gave my Angels for a reason. If I wanted to build and leave a legacy for them when the inevitable happens, what was I doing with my time to bring this to fruition? I've reaffirmed my vows and have taken control of my destiny. I will no longer rely on others to assist me in reaching my goals.

My mentor suggested a book – Eat That Frog by Author Brian Tracy which helped to tackle difficult tasks first instead of putting them off.

She is Limitless

Everyone puts tasks off occasionally, but chronic procrastinators avoid tackling complex tasks, which inevitably impacts their performance at home, in the workplace, in relationships, and overall well-being. If you are a procrastinator, break down your goals into smaller achievable tasks to make them manageable and avoid becoming overwhelmed. Find an accountability partner to help push you to ensure you act on your goals to achieve your desired life. What have you told yourself you'll complete when you have more time? What have you been putting off? For example, it could be a training program, business start-up, or a relationship. Take the following points into account:

- Procrastination prevents you from reaching your full potential
- There's no time like the present moment

Following on from this, let's take a look at the following tips:

Tips:

Set clear goals
Define what you want to accomplish and break down the tasks into smaller, manageable steps. This will help you focus on one task at a time.

Use a schedule to stay on track
Having a schedule will help you stay on track to avoid distractions. Set a timer for a certain period to work whilst taking frequent breaks. Resume working on the activity only after you have had some time out and feel refreshed.

Eliminate distractions
Identify and eliminate distractions which prevent you from working within your allocated time. For me, this includes finding a quiet workspace, turning off my phone, avoiding social media and closing unnecessary tasks on my computer.

Hold yourself accountable
Set deadlines and hold yourself responsible for meeting them. As an alternative, explore within your network of friends, family or co-workers for assistance to keep you accountable and inspired.

Reward yourself
Give yourself a treat as an incentive for completing a task or reaching a goal. Doing so will help you to stay motivated and feel good about your progress.

Take frequent breaks
When working, take a break, but be mindful of your schedule to not go over your allotted break time.

---- Chapter 8 ----
~

Redefining What Success Means to You

Success is defined differently for mothers of children with special needs than mothers without these challenges. You could benefit from redefining what success means from your own perspective. The journey of caring for a loved one with exceptional needs demands grace, patience and understanding. It's essential to let go of societal expectations and focus on what you can achieve as an individual.

Our success isn't measured according to winning accolades but by taking small steps and finding joy in the present moment. We must learn to accept what can't be changed and work through difficult times with strength, tenacity and hope. It involves adjusting to provide the best possible care alongside a welcoming, safe environment of love and acceptance. Success for mothers is about being patient, realistic, hard-working, pushing forward, learning from experiences, past mistakes and adjusting to different approaches.

More importantly, success entails being present to care for our children by providing them with the best chances for a fulfilling life. Success for the special needs child requires extra attention to care for their well-being. It could look like a newfound independence that allows for greater freedom. However, success for a family with a special needs child means something different than it does for other families. It's a complex journey that requires effort, patience, and a willingness to shift perspectives.

The redefinition of success as a special mother
Success is different to everyone, and as a special mother, success isn't about achieving perfection or meeting someone else's expectations. Instead, you may have other priorities, and it's about finding your definition of success and striving to achieve it in a way that works for you and your family. Embrace the following descriptions that differ from what society expects:

- Empowerment to take on the challenge of raising a special needs child
- Setting individual goals and standards that don't necessarily match those of other parents
- Finding moments of joy and accomplishments throughout the parenting journey
- Encouraging participation in activities that build self-confidence
- Finding ways to celebrate success
- Knowing when to ask for help from others
- Incorporating a sense of humour into parenting

She is Limitless

- Creating a support system through family and friends
- Taking the time to explore interests outside of parenting
- Taking pride in accomplishments, no matter how small

Developing a success mindset

I grew up watching my father read many books. He was a remarkable man who cherished learning about the world and was constantly seeking ways to increase his life, business, and the lives of others around him. We occasionally went to work together, and I always enjoyed sitting and listening to him speak since he had a profound insight into human behaviour. He was especially fixated on the capacity of the human intellect. One day, while spending quality time with him, he spoke about two concepts which shaped my mind and how I view the world:

1) The Placebo Effect
2) The Nocebo Effect

He began by explaining the Placebo Effect, which scientists have researched for years. The word placebo comes from Latin, meaning "I shall please." *I shall please* is the Latin root of the term placebo. One of the most popular hypotheses says that a person's expectations are what causes the placebo effect. For example, if an individual expects a pill to have a particular impact, the body's natural chemistry produces results compared to those that a specific medication might have.

Your mind is a powerful tool when given a chance. The placebo effect is a theory that's been around for a while and suggests your brain can trick your body into believing a false therapy is real to promote healing. Professor Ted Kaptchuk of Harvard-Affiliated Beth Israel Deaconess Medical Centre, whose research focuses on the placebo effect, states, *"It's about creating a stronger connection between the brain and the body and how they work together."*

My daddy was a pharmacist and frequently used scientific language to describe and explain definitions to me. For example, he explained how patients feel when they get better by taking medications, even though they have no idea what's in them or the impact it will have on their bodies. He informed me that the placebo effect was evidence of the mind's ability to influence behaviour. Some of us use medications hoping to get well to lift our spirits and bodies to produce natural chemicals that will help us feel less pain. In effect, our bodies and minds are intertwined, and what we believe impacts our overall health and mental well-being.

The Nocebo Effect on the other hand is the reverse of the placebo effect. The word "Nocebo" means "I shall harm"

She is Limitless

in Latin. It refers to a circumstance where a bad outcome happens because the intervention is harmful and referred to as the placebo effect's evil twin. It's a phenomenon that's occasionally overlooked in medication. Both of these effects are incredibly powerful. Understanding these mechanisms is vital to know how powerful your mind is and its influences on health and diseases.

For adverse reactions to medicines, nocebo implies that patients are more likely to experience a negative effect if they are worried. The adverse effects may physically impact a patient, which is often clinically diagnosable. An example of the nocebo effect is the severe effects experienced by patients taking a placebo during a clinical trial.

Furthermore, the nocebo effect significantly impacts how we perceive the world. If we are repeatedly exposed to negative messages and what is expected of us, we are more likely to lose hope in the future and become more pessimistic about it. We are less inclined to exert effort and success when we anticipate bad outcomes. This results in a self-fulfilling prophecy where negative beliefs and expectations and how they influence health or diseases become a reality.

My father continued by discussing the value of having a successful attitude, knowing that I hated studying Science in school and used some of my utterances as examples.

She is Limitless

He told me that success in life required more than talent or intelligence; it needed the ability to think strategically and concentrate on the strengths rather than the limitations, urging me to adopt a positive outlook.

Rather than saying, "I hate Maths and Physics because it's too hard," I'd change it into a positive outcome because my thoughts and beliefs influence my actions. I clung to my father's teachings from the beginning because I understood that if I had a positive attitude and worked incredibly hard, I could fulfil my dreams regardless of obstacles. My dad pushed me to question preconceived notions, seek opportunities in every circumstance, and build self-confidence.

Over the years, I've reflected on several conversations and found that my daddy imparted valuable lessons in my life. He'd tell me, "Your mindset is everything!" Although I'm still a work in progress, I learn to live by changing my thoughts and belief systems. As a professional woman raising twin girls on the autistic spectrum who suffers from epilepsy, I applied these principles, worked hard after having my first child, graduated from university with an LLM in International Commercial Law and navigated several jobs.

I've successfully pivoted my career many times, moving from Company Secretarial, a Tax Expert at HMRC, Library and Information Management, amongst many others.

She is Limitless

However, though they seemed like dream jobs at the time, I quickly grew bored of them.

A successful mindset is a way of thinking about life that emphasises achieving and capitalising on your objectives.

Accepting responsibility for your actions, understanding the bigger picture, and being aware of your skills and weaknesses are necessary for reaching your goals. Additionally, it involves adopting an optimistic mindset, taking chances and paying it forward. Finding innovative answers is an additional component of a successful mindset. Despite how challenging a situation may be, there's always a way to make it work by having faith and confidence that anything is possible when you put your mind to it.

When you define the journey on your terms, it becomes enjoyable. Creating a success roadmap helps you become more precise about your goals and is the first step in developing a mindset for greatness. Setting goals simplifies developing a strategy for achieving your objectives and inspires you to follow through. It's important to visualise your own success as it makes the goals a reality by providing a benchmark to assess your progress and adjust your strategy. As a result, you can

She is Limitless

work on your personal and professional goals. You're more likely to do something such as embark on a project when you believe you can achieve the desired result.

Don't hold yourself back, especially when you're on the cusp of a breakthrough. Doubting yourself will set you up for failure. Notwithstanding, even when you fail, remember that it's part of the process and by no means a reflection of your abilities or who you are. I'll remain positive amidst the challenging circumstances by finding ways to become the best version of myself and inspire others.

Use your failures as opportunities to learn and grow!

The lonely road to success
Some women find it difficult to stay at home as full-time carers after spending years getting a degree and investing in specific skills. These women have put in a lot of effort and worked hard over the years. They take pride in their careers and derive great satisfaction from their work. However, women with the luxury of not being in a job can choose to stay home and look after their loved ones. Being a stay-at-home mum can sometimes produce conflicting thoughts over their personal goals and the commitment to their loved ones with additional needs.

She is Limitless

It is vital that no matter which category you fall into, you should use your challenges as an opportunity to learn, improve and grow. I'd always known that being a mother is a challenging task; however, being a mother to my Twin Angels is on another level, as I realised my journey is more complicated than I envisioned. At the same time, the external pressure from family members and some well-meaning friends to stay home and care for the girls full-time is a big commitment. I would much rather spend some time working or pursuing other interests to have a more balanced life and preserve my well-being.

From the moment I accepted their diagnosis, I was determined to give them every opportunity possible to thrive and build a legacy for them; notwithstanding, it has been demanding! Working in the corporate world and balancing my caregiving role has been a rollercoaster ride. It is sometimes tempting to withdraw from companies and stressful work that no longer fulfils me, as this calling in my life isn't for the swift. After several years of accepting the status quo, I felt challenged and uncomfortable about life. I struggled to balance my responsibilities as a caregiver with my personal goals and aspirations.

It seemed I was fighting an uphill battle as I spent countless hours juggling my career with hospital appointments, leaving little time for myself or anything else. My family and friends tried to be supportive, but I

She is Limitless

struggled to maintain some relationships as I felt no one understood what I was going through. The doctors told me my Twin Angels wouldn't improve for autism even if they got the best treatment. So, I decided to fit them into my work and personal schedules whilst coping with life around their needs. The reality is that choosing to have a career or run a business whilst parenting a child who requires care is a personal choice based on our circumstances, belief system and principles.

Choosing to pursue a career or start a business is not a debatable matter of right or wrong; it's a personal choice, and you should do so if it's your passion. On the other hand, if you're a mother who intentionally chooses to be a full-time carer, make the decision without pressure from societal expectations. On the other hand, some mothers can achieve a good work-life balance by working part-time and negotiating flexible hours with their employer, allowing them to maintain their careers and care for their children simultaneously.

In April 2020, I ventured into entrepreneurship and real estate, which was extremely tough. Despite my best efforts, I didn't get anywhere with it, and for a while, part of me wanted to give up on everything else. Another part of me kept wanting to try again and pursue my dream of setting up a home care facility for individuals with autism, learning disabilities and mental health challenges.

She is Limitless

Meraki HavenCare and Rapha Haven were set up in April and June 2020, respectively. In these placements, we offer provisions for service users aged 16 years+ who work towards living independently and have needs of accommodation and support from the Local Authority or through private means. In addition, our services support users who are diagnosed with special conditions, including the following:

- ADHD
- Down syndrome
- Autism (high functioning, low needs)
- Moderate learning disabilities
- Mental health disorders
- Mild cognitive impairment

In each home, everyone has the opportunity to live life to their fullest potential and experience the best they can have with us.

> **Despite many setbacks at the onset, I've remained focused and been working tirelessly to provide my family with the best life because giving back to others fulfils me.**

Looking back on my journey, I've come a long way despite facing numerous obstacles; however, I have kept moving.

She is Limitless

The key is perseverance and consistency. I refused to give up on my dreams and decided to start small and create other opportunities. I gradually began to reframe my mindset and build a new life of habits. Although it hasn't been easy, I know the challenges made me stronger, more determined and more resilient to make a difference in the world. I am living proof there is always hope for success. Let's look at the following tips to keep you going on the journey:

Tips:

Embrace progress, not perfection
There are no blueprint or manuals for raising or caring for children, and success isn't always about achieving the perfect outcome. Instead, it's celebrating progress no matter how insignificant the result seems.

Place yourself in new and challenging situations
I knew that pushing outside my comfort zone and taking calculated risks were the keys to realising my goals and leading a meaningful life. You build confidence by overcoming obstacles but can only advance if you put yourself in new, complex situations to challenge your comfort zone.

Create a list of challenging tasks you're interested in
This can involve taking a new business course, learning new skills, travelling or launching a side hustle.

Consider failure as a chance to grow
Failure is a fantastic learning experience that signifies you can further challenge yourself with the right consistency. As an illustration, I launched a business in 2020 before COVID and lost a lot of money. Although the learning curve was steep, I now understand the need for adequate research before beginning any business venture. When we view failure as an opportunity to learn, we'll discover taking risks is easier and will make us less prone to anxiety.

Maintaining a positive attitude
Despite brief setbacks or failures, having a positive outlook while working on your goals is vital. Positive thinking entails viewing these failures as learning experiences, making moving past minor setbacks and pursuing your dreams easier. Additionally, positive thinking makes you more approachable, allowing others to help contribute to your vision. The "I can do it" mentality is an affirmation which gives a greater chance of achieving a particular goal.

Take action
Our goals are achievable, but how many of us act on them? The mindset for success calls for productive thinking, and when you consider potential barriers to reaching them, you should envision specific actions to take on board. The more quickly you can convert an idea or desire into a helpful activity, the easier it will be to get closer to your goals.

Set manageable goals
Setting small, achievable goals will help you stay on track and achieve more meaningful pursuits.

Celebrate your successes
Acknowledge the work put in and celebrate when you're making progress.

Find support
Having a network of family and friends helps you stay focused and motivated.

Practice self-care
Caring for yourself is crucial in having the energy and drive to care for your unique child. Ensure to engage in self-care practises, relax and unwind. These include reading, going for a walk or having a relaxing bath.

Ultimately, success as a special needs mother is about finding what works for you and your family. It's essential to recognise that success will look different from time to time, and that's okay. What's crucial is identifying your strengths, accepting your limitations and finding fulfilment in the small tasks. Embrace the journey, focus on your actions and remember to celebrate the small victories and progresses.

---- Chapter 9 ----
~

Breaking Barriers – Shattering Limiting Beliefs

"You begin to fly when you let go of self-limiting beliefs and allow your mind and aspirations to rise to greater heights."

Brian Tracy.

It can be easy to fall into the trap of limiting beliefs. Limiting beliefs is harmful and detrimental, preventing you from achieving your goals. They're self-deprecating fabrications we tell ourselves based on unfounded presumptions about ourselves or the environment we're surrounded in.

Limiting beliefs include thoughts such as:

- I'm not smart enough!
- I can't handle this!
- I'm not doing enough for my child!
- I'm too old!
- People won't take me seriously!

She is Limitless

Whenever we accept these beliefs, they lead to behaviours including self-sabotage and fear of failure. Limiting beliefs doesn't empower us and, in most cases, limits our potential. Unlocking your potential and leading a more fulfilling life can be achieved by letting go of limiting ideas. Many of the beliefs you currently have were due to your childhood upbringing. You base your life on the messages received by your environment. Since childhood, your internal dialogue has been shaped by these voices, primarily those of your parents, carers, teachers, mentors and the media.

Take, for instance, my fear of driving. As a child, I dreamt about being in a fatal accident and dying in a car crash. As I narrated this dream to one of my uncles the following day, he said, "Yes, you have to be extremely careful when you grow up and start driving as you can be a good driver, but others on the road may not be." As a result of his statement, the seeds of self-doubt and fear were sown.

When I was old enough and wanted to learn how to drive, I struggled with driving lesson nerves, anxiety and panic attacks behind the steering wheel and envisioned myself in a car crash when I sat at the wheel. Over the years, I formulated many reasons and explanations for my lack of confidence whilst driving. Explaining how I felt to my family and friends was difficult because they didn't understand.

She is Limitless

Finally, I realised my limiting beliefs were holding me back from achieving my goal of becoming a safe and confident driver. Firstly, I had to stop and think through my belief about driving. Next, I had to question whether the belief was true, which became the first step in breaking them down. As I developed greater self-awareness, I replaced my fear of driving with an empowering belief that I was a safe and confident driver.

In our modern era, we're greatly influenced by social media. Exposure to adverts and commercials which emphasise the importance of looking a certain way opens up the door to low self-esteem. However, most people should realise that what we see online is photoshopped, altered or airbrushed. I refused to post pictures of myself on social media for many years because I was ashamed of my body. I believed in the lie that I was fat and that social media was only for women who looked a certain way and had beautiful body features.

Through an inability to accept your own body, you expose yourself to an increased risk of developing eating disorders such as anorexia. You punish yourself with strict diets and exercise regimes. Starving yourself takes place because you're essentially starved of love. Eating disorders are symptoms of the deeper root cause – a case of inadequate self-love. I tried several diets, including the ketogenic lifestyle, Cambridge diet, south beach diet, juicing and all kinds of detoxes. However, I realised that to

She is Limitless

overcome the limiting beliefs about my body; I had to accept myself for who I was and just step into my greatness.

Recognising and addressing these beliefs is the first step to overcoming them and realising your potential. As a mother of challenged children, I had another assumption that I'd never accomplish more results or have the life I desired. I held on to this conviction as my reality and truth for most of my Twin Angels' lives. However, reading success stories about mothers in similar situations helped me accomplish my desires and shifted my perspective.

If you struggle with these issues, start by acknowledging your thoughts and feelings to overcome your limiting beliefs and ask yourself if they are true. Unfortunately, these thoughts frequently result in experiences shaping our perspective on how we see ourselves. I had to confront and challenge these thoughts and soon realised the power within to alter the trajectory of my life.

I accepted a new belief: I can still dream, take action towards my goals and achieve greatness despite difficult circumstances.

Disprove unfavourable assumptions by pointing to contrary evidence. Study people who've succeeded

She is Limitless

despite facing similar fears. In addition, talking with a therapist or supportive friend who can assist in developing a more optimistic outlook is very beneficial.

Limiting beliefs in a mother of a special needs child can include:

- Believing the child won't succeed or reach their full potential
- Believing you're the reason the child has a disability
- Believing you're solely responsible for the child's well-being and future
- Believing you're not good enough and your needs and desires are less important
- Believing you can't provide the child with the necessary care and support
- Believing you don't have enough time during the day to pursue your own goals
- Not having enough energy to pursue your goals due to feeling drained and overwhelmed

Feeling unqualified or lacking the necessary skills, education or experience to pursue your dreams is a detrimental mindset block. The notion that, as parents, we should do more for our children and feelings of being overburdened, guilty or ashamed are examples of limiting beliefs. However, for a mother of a child with special needs, it's critical to remember these emotions are normal, and their child has specific requirements catered to them.

Replace limiting beliefs with positive ones.

Once you've challenged all limiting beliefs, replace them with positive ones to support your goals and aspirations. If you've entertained limiting beliefs of not being good enough to achieve your goals, replace them with a positive belief to succeed. Engaging in constructive self-talk and focusing on your child's traits are two ways to overcome these limiting beliefs. Building supportive communities with other parents who have similar circumstances are also crucial.

Professional assistance helps create practical coping mechanisms and offers emotional support. Even though it can be challenging to control our emotions, you can still give your child the love and support they require. Letting go of limiting beliefs is critical to transforming your life and achieving your goals. Everything you need is already within you; your limiting beliefs are holding you back. Although this process requires time, effort and work, you can overcome the barriers preventing you from living your desired life with regular practice. Let's take a look at the following tips to keep you going on your journey:

Tips:

Identify your limiting beliefs
Be aware of your limiting beliefs and consider your thought patterns to pinpoint unfavourable or self-defeating thoughts preventing you from reaching your full potential. Write them down and identify the areas of your life they affect.

Challenge your limiting beliefs
Once you've identified the limiting beliefs, challenge them. Ask yourself if they're valid and if there is any proof to back them up.

Change your self-talk
Replace negative self-talk with positive affirmations which reinforce your strengths and capabilities. For example, using the phrase: "I am not good enough" and replace it with "I am capable of learning and growing in challenging environments."

Visualise your success
Visualisation is a powerful tool for overcoming limiting beliefs. Visualise yourself succeeding and achieving your dreams. Create a vision board to inspire and help you stay motivated and focused on your goals.

---- Chapter 10 ----
~

The Paralysis of Perfectionism

"The fastest way to break the cycle of perfectionism and become a fearless mother is to give up the idea of doing it perfectly – indeed, to embrace uncertainty and imperfection."

Arianna Huffington.

As part of my learning and growth, I joined a coaching academy and understood the difference between excellence and perfectionism in one of the accountability coaching sessions. In comparison, excellence is a desire to do well and produce quality work; perfectionism, on the other hand, is an unrealistic expectation to produce flawless results.

A good friend, now well-known for her delectable cakes and pastries, first discovered that perfectionism occasionally results in a lack of excellence. She once received an order for a birthday cake and worked on it for hours, focusing attentively on every detail. When the cake was delivered, the customer was upset because, despite

She is Limitless

putting so much effort into making it presentable, an essential component— its flavour—had been neglected. Due to this, she now takes time to put in her best for customers and creates the tastiest delicacies, pastries and desserts for them.

A few years ago, I participated in a mini-marathon to raise funds for a charity of my choice each year. On one 10k race to raise funds for the National Autistic Society in 2019, I was determined to run the race perfectly and set the best time. I spent months preparing and pushing myself to run faster each day. However, it didn't go as expected on the day. The weather was hot and humid, and I struggled to keep up. Instead of giving up, I stayed hydrated and focused on running my best race, regardless of the time I finished. Finally, I crossed the finish line, completely exhausted but proud of myself for giving my all to the race.

However, as much as I tried, I couldn't apply this same thought process and discipline as I began writing my book "My Journey with Twin Angels." I wanted to produce the best possible work, and whilst writing a few chapters, I convinced myself that my home wasn't perfect as I had been unable to find the ideal parenting strategies for my Angels. I didn't feel qualified to share my story with the world. I would start writing but constantly edit and re-edit, never feeling satisfied.

She is Limitless

I spent hours on single paragraphs trying to make them align. This led to a cycle of constant self-criticism, self-doubt and anxiety. I felt that my friends and family were watching and would point fingers and accuse me of trying to be something I wasn't. Finally, after joining the coaching academy and stumbling upon an article about overcoming perfectionism, I decided to finish my first draft and set a deadline. I committed to writing a certain number of words each day. Slowly but surely, I began to see progress. My first draft was far from perfect, but I had been able to complete it, and that was far more than I'd ever achieved.

I started letting go of my need for flawless perfection and began embracing my imperfections.

I reminded myself that it was not final and could always go back and revise. Yet, with my newfound mindset, I still struggled. On some days, I'd step back and remind myself why I was writing in the first place. I wanted to turn my mess into a message and share my journey to help others. Ultimately, completing the book took me over ten years of battling perfectionism! Expecting yourself to be perfect in every way obstructs your path to greater self-love.

Through wanting to be perfect, you strive to be at the top, error-free and produce impeccable work. However, you will invariably find your set standards unattainable if they are over-realistic. For this reason, discontentment sets in, and the agony is endless because you're never delighted with your actions, behaviours or achievements. You're in the perpetual state of feeling incomplete and unfulfilled.

There is nothing wrong with wanting to produce fine work or hoping to project a positive image of yourself. However, having a perfectionistic streak has unfavourable consequences. Whilst striving for perfection can be viewed positively, it harms our mental health and well-being. Because you expect perfection, you are harsh towards yourself and easily fall into judgement mode. You risk losing perspective in pursuing perfection because you fear losing out. You find that fear prevents you from taking action, and you only start to act when the environment is perfect and easy.

Understand the difference between:

'Pursuing perfectionism' and the 'desire for excellence.'

Perfectionism is an unattainable goal. The pursuit of excellence is a far superior course of action. You're continuously improving and aiming to produce great work in the spirit of excellence.

When you learn to love yourself, you don't punish your mind with unkind thoughts and judgements. Instead, learn to accept the flaws and make them work for you. As a result, you're willing to forgive yourself more readily. Here are some examples of how perfectionism can have an impact on us:

Anxiety and stress
Perfectionists frequently establish impossible standards for themselves, which cause them to feel pressure and anxiety. This also leads to excessive planning, often leading to chronic burnout. Be mindful of this because nothing is worth stressing over because you're always a work-in-progress.

Low self-esteem
Perfectionists make you feel inadequate or unworthy because of the intense self-criticism when one doesn't fulfil their standards. This can lead to a negative self-image and a lack of self-confidence.

Relationship problems
Perfectionists have unrealistic expectations of others, leading to disappointment, anger and frustration when their standards aren't met. They also struggle with vulnerability and intimacy, fearing their loved ones will expose their flaws and shortcomings and find it difficult to accept constructive criticism or admit mistakes.

Decreased productivity

Perfectionists spend time on one task to ensure it's perfect, which leads to low results and procrastination. They have an issue delegating tasks to others because they believe they can handle everything themselves. We must recognise the harmful effects of perfectionism and the lack of delegation and embrace the beauty of balance for excellent results. We can manage perfectionism by asking for help from friends, family or a mental health expert to minimise the impact on our overall well-being. Let's look at the following tips on how to minimise perfectionism:

Tips:

Embrace your mistakes

Recognise that perfectionism is impossible to achieve. Everyone makes mistakes, and faults are a normal part of learning. For this reason, make sure you embrace the errors and improve for better results.

Challenge your perfectionist-thoughts

Challenge your black-and-white thinking whenever you catch yourself doing so with alternative viewpoints. Learning from others' perspectives is a healthy way of dealing with challenges because they may suggest an idea you hadn't thought of, which could benefit you in the long run.

She is Limitless

Focus on progress, not perfection
Set attainable, challenging and realistic goals rather than aiming for perfectionism. Acknowledge and celebrate your progress, even if it's not perfect. Doing so will help you build confidence internally and with others.

Avoid overthinking
Overthinking leads to analytical paralysis. Instead, concentrate on taking action, moving forward, enjoying the journey and making gradual progress.

Accept feedback from others
Feedback can be tough to receive; however, it's essential for our growth and development. Learn to accept feedback without taking it personally.

Seek help
If you're struggling with perfectionism, consider getting treatment from a professional. A therapist can support you in coping mechanisms and offer support as you work to overcome perfectionism. Remember that overcoming perfectionism takes time and effort, and as you attempt to adopt a healthier and balanced way of life, be patient and kind to yourself.

---- Chapter 11 ----
~

Unmasking Imposter Syndrome – *when you know you're ENOUGH!*

"When you stop focusing on all things that you're not. When you stop fussing over perceived flaws. When you remove all imposed and unbelievable expectations on yourself. When you start celebrating yourself more. When you focus on all that you are. When you start believing that your perceived flaws are just that – perception."

Malebo Sephodi.

I desire to become a famous writer and own multiple businesses, but it can sometimes be overwhelming as a mother of twins who require around-the-clock care. There were moments when I second-guessed myself if I had what it took to succeed. Suddenly, my life was consumed with doctor's appointments, therapy sessions and caregiving duties, and I decided to put my dreams on hold to focus on my Angels' needs.

She is Limitless

As the years went by, I watched from the sidelines as my friends and acquaintances achieved success in their careers and businesses. I felt as if I was falling behind and opened myself to doubt, constantly challenged by my abilities, wondering if I was called for entrepreneurship or if I was being delusional.

After a dinner date with a friend, I started writing again. As I began to write, I felt that other qualified writers and bloggers seemed to know what they were doing while I was pretending. As the weeks, months and years passed, imposter syndrome invited itself unexpectedly. I would spend hours writing blog posts, and no matter how hard I tried, I couldn't shake the feeling that I wasn't good enough in my writing abilities.

I felt unqualified, started speaking with other special mums, and realised I wasn't alone in feeling this way. We all deal with imposter syndrome at some point in our lives. I realised everyone was doing their best and started to believe that my dreams were possible and that I could achieve success to be a great mum to my children and family.

Imposter syndrome is a familiar feeling of self-doubt or inadequacy, where one feels like a fraud, despite having accomplished significant achievements. Special needs mums often experience imposter syndrome due to the constant pressure of raising children with additional needs.

Mothers of children with special needs juggling numerous obligations and challenges whilst providing for their children can overcome imposter syndrome. Below are suggestions on what mothers can do to minimize negative thought patterns and adopt a healthy mindset:

Recognise and acknowledge your feelings
The first step in conquering imposter syndrome is recognising your feelings. It's critical to understand that you're not alone in having these emotions, as they are common to all. Be gentle with yourself and speak directly to that imposter telling it who you are and all the achievements you've received so far.

Make friends with other special needs mothers
Developing friendships with other mums with special needs children is a great way to build a warm and friendly environment of supportive people to bring new perspectives. By joining a support group or attending a local meetup, you can exchange experiences and learn from others.

Concentrate on what you do best
Focus on your strengths rather than your shortcomings, weaknesses, or areas where you feel inadequate. List all your strengths, what you're good at and your

accomplishments. Learn to celebrate your successes and remind yourself of them on a daily basis to keep you going.

Change negative perceptions
When you have doubts about yourself or your abilities, confront them with evidence to the contrary. For instance, if you think you're not qualified for a job, remind yourself of your skills and experience and remember that you didn't study for a degree or qualification, for it to go to waste.

Speak with others
Talk about your feelings with people you trust and provide support and encouragement when they go through similar emotions.

Recognise that you're not alone
Imposter syndrome affects many people and is a common feeling among high achievers. Remember, you can talk to people around you and share the load.

Identify and challenge negative thoughts
When you experience imposter syndrome, you may have negative thoughts about yourself. The first action step is to identify and challenge these thoughts by asking yourself if they are based on facts or assumptions.

She is Limitless

Celebrate your successes
Take the time to reflect on your achievements and the hard work invested. Celebrate your successes no matter how small they seem.

Don't compare yourself to others
Avoid comparing yourself to others; remember that everyone has unique strengths, flaws, and shortcomings.

Focus on your learning, growth and development
Instead of perfectionism, focus on your learning, growth and development. This helps you to accept obstacles as opportunities to learn and improve.

Seek support
By sharing your feelings with a trusted confidant, you're able to receive support and gain a new perspective from another source. Imposter syndrome is a feeling that can't be trusted because it is not your identity. That said, you can overcome imposter syndrome and reach your fullest potential whilst learning from others. No one can do life alone – reach out to someone.

---- Chapter 12 ----
~

Speaking Life and the Power of the Mind

"The secret of a better and more successful life is to cast out those old, dead, unhealthy thoughts. Substitute for them new, vital, dynamic faith-thoughts. You can depend on it – an inflow of new thoughts will remake you and your life."

Norman Vincent Peale.

If you've come to this part of the book, I want to encourage you to dream bigger and increase your determination to achieve every goal set out for you. Pursuing your interests takes courage, strength, and resilience, especially when juggling many responsibilities. Positive thinking is a powerful tool that helps special mothers stay focused on their dreams and aspirations.

Looking on the bright side of life and emphasising the positive aspects of our circumstances are key examples of positive thinking. You can think positively by adopting an attitude of gratitude, surrounding yourself with positive people, and highlighting the brighter sides of every circumstance. Special mothers who adopt a positive approach reduce stress, increase motivation and encourage self-care activities. You are able to solve challenges creatively by using positive thinking to help in approaching situations with an open mind.

Your thoughts shape your reality, and whilst positive thinking isn't the complete solution to overcome imposter syndrome, it can help build consistent resilience and a sense of purpose. Let's look at the following tips on how to discipline our speech and thoughts in tough times:

Tips:

Focus on what you can control
As special mothers, we face situations beyond our control. Concentrating on what we have control over makes us more empowered and less overwhelmed.

Honour the little victories and accomplishments
Whether it's a therapeutic breakthrough or just getting through a challenging day, acknowledging and celebrating these successes helps to build momentum and create a sense of progress.

Develop an attitude of thankfulness
Gratitude is a powerful strategy for shifting your perspective from what you don't have to what you do have. Spending time each day to reflect on your blessings

and what you're grateful for helps to shift your mindset to a positive state.

Surround yourself with positive people
Find positive influences in your life, whether they're friends, family members or support groups. Depending on the nature and consistency of the relationships, these individuals will be able to offer support and provide encouragement to help you stay motivated and focused on your goals.

Create a vision board
Take time each day to visualise yourself achieving every dream written down. Whether it's envisioning yourself giving a successful presentation or graduating with a degree, creating a vision board represents your accomplishments and helps you stay motivated on your goals.

Refrain from negative thinking
Negative thinking focuses on what isn't going well, delaying your progress. It harms a mother's mental health and well-being, causing anxiety, pessimism, poor self-esteem and depression, which makes it difficult whilst parenting a special needs child.

Negative thinking can be avoided by adding value to your current relationships, improving your speech and investing in your physical well-being. In addition, it's crucial to cultivate thankfulness for life's beautiful moments. As a special mother, you may have encountered the following patterns when dealing with your children and life in general:

Catastrophising

Catastrophising involves preparing for the worst. For instance, special needs mothers may think they can't achieve anything because they're too occupied with caring for their unique children.

Overgeneralising

This often involves taking one negative experience and using that as the reason for not moving forwards. This is dangerous as it increases complacency and encourages laziness.

All-or-nothing thinking

This involves viewing a situation from a positive or negative place with no room for compromise. For example, a special needs mum may believe that if she can't provide for her child's needs, it makes her a failure as a mother.

Blaming yourself

This often involves taking personal responsibility for circumstances outside of one's control.

Discounting the positives
This involves downplaying positive experiences and accomplishments. For example, a special mum may underestimate her achievements because she thinks they're insignificant compared to her children's challenges. Let's take a look at the following tips on how to overcome negative challenges:

Tips:

How to quiet your negative inner voice
These harmful thought patterns need to be recognised and challenged by special mothers. However, there are vital tools mothers can implement, including:

Exercising and taking breaks
Exercise can make you feel less stressed and tense, which is beneficial for reducing negative thoughts. Taking frequent breaks throughout the day will help clear your mind from distractions.

Connect with yourself
Take time to focus on your inner thoughts and emotions. Pause and ask yourself, "How am I feeling?'" This can help to identify the sources of negative thoughts and allow you to work through them.

She is Limitless

Meditation
Take slow deep breaths and allow yourself to focus on connecting with the Divine. Whenever I am in God's Presence, I have a great sense of tranquillity and peace. This practice nurtures my soul and deepens my connection with Him. If you do this, you'll have more control over your thoughts which influences your life.

Talk to yourself positively
Focus on the positive aspects of yourself and lean into how much you've accomplished so far.

Engage in self-care activities
These include activities such as reading, meditating, music or talking to friends, which helps you to relax and re-focus your mind.

Spend time shifting your perspective
Reframing your thoughts helps you to see from a different perspective in a more positive light.

Make an intentional decision to stay in the present moment
Staying in the present moment will help to reduce the negative thoughts about where you should be right now. Lean into what each day reveals and embrace the current lessons.

She is Limitless

Use humour as a coping mechanism
Laughing at yourself and the experiences will help to reduce stress and anxiety.

Create an affirmation mantra
Positive self-talk helps to reduce negative self-esteem and, therefore, empowers you.

Challenge yourself
Taking on new challenges helps to boost self-confidence in your abilities.

Get creative
Expressing yourself through creative outlets such as art, music and writing will increase your mindset and put you to ease.

Get enough sleep
Engaging in healthy sleeping habits will help to improve your mood.

Believe that all things are possible
Having faith that anything is possible is a scriptural reference I love, which can be found in Matthew 19:26. While getting discouraged and having negative thoughts is easy, it doesn't have to define a mother's experience or outlook. It's essential to understand that one needs to work ahead with the belief that no matter how many hurdles come, it's still possible to persevere.

She is Limitless

---- Chapter 13 ----
~

Recognising the Value of Self-Empowerment

"No one can make you feel inferior without your consent."

Eleanor Roosevelt.

Your family's well-being will depend on how intentional you are with investing in your own. This means you must step out of your comfort zone to gain knowledge, skills and confidence to take control over your life. Your sense of self-worth and confidence in your capacity to care for your loved one and achieve other objectives increases due to empowering yourself. It helps to manage the emotional inconsistencies about caring for a child with additional needs.

Prioritising your needs and focusing on what makes you happy and fulfilled will significantly improve your ability to control stress and keep a positive outlook. A woman who is confident in her abilities takes charge of her life, makes independent choices and accepts responsibility for her happiness and success.

She is Limitless

She has faith in her skills and understands her power within to work for the life she desires. Furthermore, she demonstrates that taking chances and failing leads to growth and learning; thus, she's not scared to do either!

As a special mum, it's vital to understand the concept of self-empowerment and how it positively impacts our lives. It's about confidence, taking charge of your life, choices and actions.

Self-empowerment is crucial as it lowers stress and minimises the risk of burnout.

Due to the unique daily obstacles of the special mum, life can become overwhelming. For this reason, being self-empowered makes prioritising your well-being easier to focus on solutions rather than problems. You see challenges as opportunities for growth and development and become a role model to provide an excellent example for your family to emulate.

Additionally, they'll grow from your example and gain confidence to develop greater independence and self-assurance. Let's focus on the positive traits of a self-empowered woman:

She is Limitless

She is limitless
Her intellect is a vast universe of endless possibilities, and she constantly seeks to broaden her horizons and challenge herself. She personifies strength and resilience. She is unshakable in her resolve; a fire that fuels her ambitions and refuses to settle for mediocrity. Failure is simply a stepping stone; an opportunity to evolve and learn. She recognises that success is determined by how much she embraces her true potential rather than societal expectations. She is limitless because she believes in herself, capabilities and power to make a difference. She smashes the glass ceilings that bring constrain, opening the way for a future where limitations are mere illusions.

She is self-aware
A self-empowered woman is aware of her values, strengths and flaws. She knows what she wants and is prepared to put effort into achieving her goals.

She is resilient
She is capable of recovering from disappointments and setbacks. She doesn't hesitate to express her opinions, take chances, or attempt new tasks or projects.

She is independent
She is comfortable being alone and isn't reliant on others for her happiness or success. She is capable of making independent choices and accepting responsibility for the results.

She is Limitless

She is empathetic
An empowered woman has empathy for other people and understands the viewpoints of others by placing herself in their position.

She is open-minded
She is often open to new ideas and perspectives. She is unafraid to question her convictions and willing to pick up new ideas to learn from others. A self-empowered woman isn't perfect; however, she's ready to take responsibility for her own life and adjust when necessary. She understands true empowerment comes from within and has the ability to create the life she wants. She serves and inspires others through her actions and is a role model for women who aspire to empower themselves.

Remember that self-empowerment is a journey, not a destination. Let's continue with the following tips on how women can embrace the beauty of self-empowerment:

Tips:

Develop a positive self-image
Start with discovering how to accept and love yourself for who you are. Recognise the unique traits which make you who you are, including your strengths and limitations.

She is Limitless

Set clear boundaries
Establish boundaries and stick to them. This will help communicate your needs and wants to others while safeguarding your emotional and physical well-being.

Believe in yourself
Trust your abilities and have confidence in your decisions. Don't be afraid to take risks and pursue your goals.

Learn to say 'No!'
Saying no to offers or suggestions that don't serve or align with your values shouldn't make you feel bad. You have the right to prioritise your needs and refuse requests.

Continuously learn and grow
Accept new challenges, learn new skills and push yourself to step out of your comfort zone. You will develop and improve as a result by becoming the best version of yourself.

---- Chapter 14 ----
~

Empowering through Wellness and Self-Care

"Self-care is how you take your power back."

Lalah Delia.

The Oxygen Mask safety speech is a routine part of the boarding process for anyone seated on a plane. Frequently, it falls into the background as we adjust ourselves in preparation for several hours in the sky. Nonetheless, the speech carries a beautiful message regarding self-care.

The Oxygen Mask Rule is simple: "If the cabin loses pressure, oxygen masks will fall from above. You are to put your mask on first before helping others." For parents, this may seem somewhat unbelievable, but we want to protect our children and feel the urge to forget our masks while securing theirs. This instinct reflects a common occurrence in the daily lives of many parents. The problem with breaking the Oxygen Mask Rule is that we increase the risk to our health and those relying on us to keep them safe.

She is Limitless

Why is this an important rule for ensuring survival?
If you run out of oxygen, you can't help anyone with their own mask. This is an essential metaphor for those who spend much of their time caring for others, including mothers, fathers, caregivers, doctors, nurses, and teachers. Unfortunately, taking care of others can quickly deplete the caregiver. If you don't take care of yourself, you will experience burnout, stress, fatigue, reduced mental effectiveness, health problems, anxiety, frustration and the inability to sleep. Are you experiencing any of these symptoms right now?

Caregivers must be replenished and preserve their energy to continue caring for others. Self-care is crucial for everyone's well-being. It's something that isn't to be taken for granted as an extraordinary mother. Caring for a child with special needs is physically and emotionally draining. Neglecting your own needs leads to burnout, stress and other health issues. For this reason, you need to check in with yourself, know when to unwind and develop good routines that promote well-being.

You may find yourself juggling various responsibilities, including managing your loved one's medical needs, attending appointments, advocating for your child's rights and managing emotional challenges in raising a child with additional needs. Taking care of yourself is essential not only for your own well-being but to give you the ability to care for your child. When you feel overwhelmed, providing the level of care your child needs can be challenging.

To practice self-care, you must identify your own needs and have balance. This consists of:

- Eating healthy
- Going to dinner with friends
- Working out frequently
- Getting adequate sleep
- Taking breaks from screens including mobile phones and laptops (social media to be precise!)
- Meditating
- Writing in a journal
- Participating in hobbies
- Reading

We cultivate resilience and positivity by engaging in self-care, practising gratitude, and connecting with our inner selves. Even though setting aside time for self-care reaps many benefits, taking care of ourselves costs money and time.

Self-care is vital for our welfare, both physically and mentally, and is why we should schedule time for it on a daily basis. In addition, by taking self-care seriously and making it a priority, we are refuelled and better equipped to handle life's obstacles as they come.

She is Limitless

Self-care for a mother of a child with special needs is self-love that confirms our value as people who deserve to take time to look after themselves. Doing so controls several stress levels, elevates our mood, lessens our anxiety, and enhances our well-being.

Types of self-care
Self-care strategies vary depending on the individual. Something as simple as practising deep breathing for 5 minutes significantly impacts our mental health. Therefore, it's crucial to identify the activities which suit your needs and strike a balance among the various forms of self-care. Self-care takes many forms, and choosing one which suits you best is critical. The most popular self-care regimes include the following:

Physical self-care
For a special mum, physical self-care is crucial. Spend time relaxing, eating healthy foods, working out, and caring for your mental and emotional well-being. Talk to your family and friends, and if you need it, get professional assistance. Concentrate on getting enough sleep and exercising to produce more energy. Meditate and schedule breaks throughout the day to set aside time for hobbies, including artmaking and journaling. Prioritising relationships build genuine connections and a friendly, supportive group. Doing this lets you keep in touch with loved ones and reach out to them occasionally.

She is Limitless

Mental self-care

Physical and mental self-care work collectively. Maintaining your optimism and attention to what makes you happy is critical, and this is done through spending time to clear your mind and concentrate on mindful exercises, including breathing, writing and meditation. My most joyful moments are giving back to the community, connecting with friends and family and participating in activities that make me feel good. In addition, numerous resources are available to assist with mental health issues that need to be dealt with graciously. Moreover, you're able to develop a healthy mindset through journaling and reading a book in the current season you're in.

Social self-care

Social self-care is crucial for preserving healthy relationships and overall well-being. Make contact with your loved ones and schedule quality time for enlightening conversations. Engage in moments that make you happy. For those who like sports, music, art and movies, make sure you participate in these activities often. Participate in your neighbourhood's activities and offer spare time to speaking engagements that elevate the community. As much as it's crucial to be a beacon of light around others, we must also be mindful that we don't take on more than we can bear. Investing in others should be balanced to avoid burnout and provide your best care to yourself and those around you.

Emotional self-care

For one to stay mentally balanced, emotional self-care is essential. Be aware of your emotions to ensure they don't overwhelm your mind, and find ways to cope with the mechanisms. There are healthy ways to express your feelings and build healthy relationships with others. Talk to loved ones, seek counselling or therapy for emotional support, keep a journal, and engage in prayer and meditation. To build a healthy state of emotional well-being, emphasise kind words and self-compassion within your environment. In addition to this, let's talk about the benefits of self-care:

Benefits of self-care:

Self-care enhances focus

You are able to concentrate better when you're not overwhelmed as you gain clarity and focus more on the present moment. When you are at ease and your body is calm, your focus sharpens, and you become productive in your personal and professional endeavours.

Boosts productivity

People who regularly practice self-care are more likely to have productive results because they have a better cognitive level and can focus on more in-depth discussions. In addition, these people plan their days effectively and rid their minds of unnecessary clutter, which promotes a better work-life balance.

She is Limitless

How to maintain a healthy self-care schedule:
- Set realistic goals and expectations for yourself
- Make time for activities that are relaxing and enjoyable
- Exercise regularly
- Develop healthy nutritional habits
- Get plenty of rest and sleep
- Spend enjoyable time with loved ones and friends
- Enjoy outdoor activities and maintain connection to nature
- Make time for creative activities or hobbies
- Engage in activities which advance your knowledge
- Schedule time each day to indulge in enjoyable activities
- Prioritise self-care in your daily routines
- Journal your thoughts and feelings
- Examine your life and note several areas which require consistent improvement
- Choose self-care habits you love that are in alignment with what you believe in
- Remain adaptable and be open to adjustments
- Develop a positive attitude towards yourself and life
- Seek professional assistance
- Adopt the right mindset
- Embrace change and be open to taking risks
- Celebrate your success and accomplishments
- Stay consistent*
- Measure and track your progress

She is Limitless

Self-care tips

Mothers of children with special needs experience guilt when they take time off. They might think they're neglecting their child for not doing enough. Mothers must learn to take care of themselves for the following reasons:

Reduction of stress and anxiety

Stress and anxiety can show among mothers of special needs children. The solution to avoid these pitfalls is taking care of yourself and managing each day as it comes.

Improvement in your relationships

Healthy connections with family and friends are fostered by emphasising self-care activities, including exercise, meditation, journaling, massages, or reading.

Maintaining your physical health

Taking time for physical activities, including walking, swimming, or cycling, helps to maintain and promote good health.

Improve your ability to handle difficult emotions

Managing challenging situations is the ability to test your mental strength and still keep going, despite being overwhelmed or feeling like a failure. For this reason, it is important to be open about your weaknesses and set healthy boundaries to know when to seek help and when to work on yourself individually.

Boost self-confidence
Dedicate quality time to work on a task or project you enjoy and learn to invest in new methods to build your own self-confidence.

Prioritise your own needs
When we put our own needs first, we are able to prioritise and meet the needs of others more effectively.

Increase energy levels
Filling your cup before caring for others will help you remain invigorated for the task.

Promote better sleep
You can improve your sleep by creating a relaxing and tranquil environment, maintaining a regular bedtime routine, and reducing exposure to coffee, nicotine and alcohol.

Practice self-compassion
Self-compassion is developed by being kind to yourself and realising that mistakes are learning experiences.

Improve your decision-making
Frequently pausing, taking breaks and checking in with yourself helps to make better decisions in challenging situations.

She is Limitless

Create a better environment for your child
Self-care helps your loved ones thrive in supportive environments.

Connecting with others
Joining support groups and connecting with other parents in similar situations can help provide emotional support.

Foster creativity
Exploring creative outlets including painting, writing, or crafting can foster creativity in other areas of your life.

Increase satisfaction in your work
Self-care can help you feel energised and motivated to complete tasks more efficiently.

To maintain balance in life
Before agreeing to other people's demands, consider whether doing so will help you stay balanced and if it aligns with your beliefs.

Decrease your risk of depression
Your risk of developing depression can be lowered by scheduling time for self-care activities, including adequate sleep, exercising, or eating a balanced and healthy diet.

Refocus on your self-care routines
Taking a break to re-focus can help you become more mindful and attentive in your interactions with others. As

She is Limitless

a special needs mum, you face unique challenges that impact your well-being. However, prioritising wellness and self-care puts you in a better position to negotiate several hurdles despite the obstacles. Self-care is not selfish; it's essential for your well-being and maintaining a healthy balance when caring for a child with special needs. It's a requirement, not a luxury. Activities including self-care tools, journaling and creating vision boards are intended to help you become unstoppable. Write down your favourite self-care activities:

_____
_____
_____
_____
_____
_____
_____
_____
_____
_____
_____
_____
_____
_____

---- Chapter 15 ----
~

Self-Help and Coping Strategies

"Don't start your day with the broken pieces of yesterday. Every day is a fresh start. Each day is a new beginning. Every morning we wake up is the first day of our new life."

Author Unknown.

Just before the COVID-19 pandemic, I started several businesses to provide a better life for my family. However, I lost thousands of pounds, and in addition to my caregiving role, it nearly made me suicidal. I hit rock bottom and suffered a mental breakdown. All this happened amidst friends and family, and my silent pleas for help went unnoticed. For this reason, I knew it was time to get serious help.

I forgave myself for investing large amounts of money into a business I wasn't familiar with and stopped hiding my feelings. I was angry, sad and bitter for a long time, but when I finally admitted that I was unhappy with my circumstances, I started seeking help and made gradual changes. It felt liberating to finally let go of the negative feelings and replace them with positive energy.

I asked for help, but could only do that once I'd accepted to finally let go of the feelings and emotions. Self-help is the practice of taking control of your well-being.

Higher self-awareness, greater self-confidence, improved problem-solving skills, increased creativity and spiritual development are benefits of self-help. It's crucial to remember that self-help is a process which takes time to experience.

Nevertheless, it's helpful to pinpoint problem areas, investigate solutions and sources of assistance and implement a strategy for improvement. Remember to appreciate your accomplishments thus far. Investing in yourself will improve your well-being and help to achieve your potential.

Benefits of self-help
Make time for enjoyment and schedule it regularly so you can engage in activities such as going to the park, playing games, and spending quality time with the family. Mums with special needs children can practise self-care techniques, including meditation, prayer, exercise, and eating a balanced diet. Let's take a look at the following tips to enhance your self-help routines:

Tips:

Nurture healthier relationships
Mums can use self-help techniques to improve their relationships with others. Learning to listen actively and respecting other people's opinions is necessary. Additionally, it entails setting boundaries, managing expectations and learning from past mistakes. As a result, self-help strategies enable people to develop emotional intelligence, forge closer relationships with others and become more aware of their wants and desires.

Improve your self-awareness
Self-help techniques can be used to increase self-awareness. This entails exercises such as journaling and reflection. Studying thoughts and feelings can provide insights into how they affect and interact with one's life and relationships. You are also able to discover new hobbies and engage in activities that increase self-awareness, assist individuals in recognising their strengths and limitations, and help to comprehend the motivations underlying their actions.

Identify and focus on your personal objectives
Self-help assists special mothers in determining and concentrating on their objectives. Setting reasonable expectations and creating detailed plans to achieve these objectives help immensely. It could also entail exploring innovative approaches to problems. Self-help techniques

include reassessing one's progress regularly to ensure goals are accomplished within a specific timeframe. The mother of a child with special needs can improve her wellness and set the foundation for a happy future by taking the time to concentrate on personal objectives and working towards them.

Boosting self-confidence and self-esteem
To boost your self-confidence and self-esteem, you must take action to engage in meaningful tasks you can be proud of. This goes beyond simply changing how you think and behave toward yourself and leads to improved self-confidence, inspiring other successful endeavours. For example, utilising positive affirmations, setting realistic goals and engaging in constructive self-talk. From a practical perspective, self-help techniques include the following:

- Looking back on prior achievements
- Learning from errors
- Concentrating on your strengths rather than the shortcomings

It also entails identifying strengths and weaknesses and finding strategies to improve them. By committing to a self-help practice, people are able to increase their self-confidence and have a more positive attitude towards their lives.

Self-help makes you more empowered

By developing a self-help plan, you maintain control over your life. Coping mechanisms are approaches to managing stress, anxiety, and difficult situations. They can be proactive or reactive, including speaking to reliable friends, working out, maintaining a journal, and enjoying activities. Proactive and reactive strategies are categorised into two primary groups including:

1) **Proactive** – addressing the underlying causes of stress. This entails taking proactive measures such as looking for a solution, changing your environment, or shifting viewpoints.

2) **Reactive** – reactive coping mechanisms include exercise, mindfulness and relaxation techniques; to name a few.

There's no one-size-fits-all method for managing stress. Everyone has different coping strategies that are effective for them. Therefore, it's crucial to experiment with the most effective in any given circumstance. In addition, we should recognise and avoid harmful coping strategies such as substance misuse or self-harm and get professional help when necessary.

Develop a support system

Speak with close friends and other parents going through similar experiences to receive advice, encouragement, support, and practical assistance. A support network can help a mother of a child with special needs in performing daily duties such as focusing on their loved one's medical needs, education and assistance in providing emotional support. A robust support system enables the mother to concentrate on her own needs and those of her family, giving everyone a sense of stability and comfort.

Remain organised
Any parent who has children with special needs may find it challenging to maintain organisation and structure. Establishing a manageable schedule that works for your family is crucial. You can start by choosing a specific home chore to complete by setting a timeframe for certain activities for you and your family to unwind and spend quality time together. Additionally, it can be difficult to remember appointments, school activities, therapies and other essential details. For this reason, use a calendar, online resources, mobile apps or other tools to stay organised to ensure you get the important dates and deadlines on time.

Consult a professional
Consider going to individual or family counselling to receive support. There are several advantages for families with special needs who require help to receive expert assistance. Working with qualified professionals will help you understand your child's requirements, develop effective behavioural management techniques, and care

for psychological or emotional disorders. In addition, professionals will help ensure that your child receives the finest care possible by creating educational plans and accessing necessary resources.

Find resources
Finding practical and emotional support for your family can be difficult and emotionally draining. Parents of children with special needs may find a sense of connection and understanding by looking for local support groups. Finding internet sources and forums can be helpful because they give access to trustworthy information and offer support when needed. By carving out time for something you enjoy, you'll easily tend to your personal needs. Research neighbourhood associations, institutions of higher learning and other sources for assistance and information.

Advocate for your loved ones
Do thorough research on your child's privileges and rights so you can advocate for them when necessary. Advocating for your child is vital to ensuring success and gaining the resources and services required to meet their needs. This includes attending meetings with teachers and doctors, looking for beneficial programs and services, and speaking out to uphold your child's needs and rights. Additionally, remaining informed about changes and additions to local laws and regulations will help to defend your child's rights.

She is Limitless

Take a break
Spend time with people you love and indulge in your interests. A special mother can benefit from taking a break and using it as an opportunity to gain perspective and engage in self-care. It's an excellent way for parents to think about their actions and how it impacts their children to develop new strategies and engage with them.

Create a routine which works
Establishing a routine is one of the best ways to support yourself as a mother of a child with special needs. It gives a sense of direction and a framework for organising daily interactions and activities. Routines give children a sense of security, reducing their anxiety and allowing them to exercise self-control and improve their communication skills.

Be open-minded
Being adaptable is crucial for mothers of children with special needs. For this reason, flexibility lets parents alter their strategies in response to their children's circumstances, conditions, and behaviours. Flexibility helps to promote spontaneity and relaxation. Establishing a healthy environment for parents and children makes it easier for everyone in the family.

Build your village
Don't assume you need to go through these challenges alone. Now is the time to network and find your tribe to

establish your village, which means finding others on a similar journey with you. Join online or special needs communities to keep you informed and involved. Within your village, you are able to find a safe space to vent your frustrations, seek solace, openly celebrate milestones, and share resources and assistance when needed.

It's helpful to connect with other parents going through similar experiences, join online communities, or contact experts, including therapists or social workers. Mothers can raise awareness for the needs and rights of their loved ones by working together and using their collective voices. Interactions with other families will give children a sense of community and belonging, which benefits them.

Celebrate progress
No matter how small your child has achieved a task, acknowledge and applaud their accomplishments to keep them motivated. This also applies to mothers with special needs children. For example, a mother of a child with special needs can be motivated to identify progress by how she resonates and relates to the child. Celebrations can take many forms, such as hosting a party or creating a unique craft. Participating in activities allows people to bond and create lasting memories while recognising accomplishments.

She is Limitless

Set realistic expectations
Be gentle with yourself and your child. Be flexible and willing to make mistakes. Setting realistic targets can benefit the mother of a child with special needs whilst encouraging accountability and assisting in the development of structure and clarity. At the same time, it's essential to manage these expectations, be adaptive, comprehend adjustments and keep your expectations reasonable and easy to meet.

Request assistance
Don't be afraid to seek help when you need it. For the mother of a child with special needs, asking for assistance is the crucial first step. Getting help from experts such as therapists or social workers is beneficial. In addition to this, let's look at the following copies strategies to help mothers develop a positive mindset with their special needs children.

Identify triggers
Determine situations, people and events that make you feel uncomfortable and find ways to solve them in a healthy manner.

Talk it out
Speak with a family member or friend you can trust to talk to about your emotions.

She is Limitless

Write it out
Gain perspective and clarity by putting your ideas and feelings on paper.

Take breaks
Give yourself regular breaks from demanding situations so you have time to unwind.

Exercise
Endorphins are hormones released during exercise that help reduce stress and boost mood.

Eat well
Maintain your energy and focus by eating a healthy balanced diet.

Get enough sleep
Having enough sleep allows your body and mind to rejuvenate.

Take time for yourself
Spending time to engage in activities will enable you to unwind and rest.

Practice mindfulness
Being mindful involves embracing and not passing judgement on yourself or your emotions. Take it one day at a time and be kind to yourself whilst discovering what suits you the best.

---- Chapter 16 ----
~

Owning your Ideal Life

If you're tired of living a life that no longer serves you, it's time to start creating the life you envision! You can make your dreams come true, whether to travel the world, launch your own business or spend more time with your loved ones.

Question: Do you feel ready to take control over your life and create a future you're passionate about?

For many years, I operated on autopilot; for those following my journey, you'd know I often felt overwhelmed and exhausted from the relentless responsibilities of caring for my Twin Angels. I wasn't living – I was going through the motions each day and became weary and frustrated. I realised it was time to regain control over my life. I have a strong passion for writing, and I continue developing my abilities in the therapeutic expression of words which makes me very happy.

She is Limitless

It is tough juggling everything as I am still a caregiver; my role is not going away. Despite this, I've chosen to persevere because I know by sharing my story and encouraging those around me, anything is possible as long as there is a willingness to learn. A life that aligns with my beliefs, interests, and purpose is what it means to "design a life I love." It involves thinking about what matters the most and making a plan to achieve it.

But where do you start?
Let's look at the following practical steps:

Determine your core values
What holds the biggest significance in your life? What do you desire to prioritise? Write your core values which includes anything from freedom, to creativity, family or something entirely different:

_____
_____
_____
_____
_____
_____
_____
_____

She is Limitless

Envision the life you want

After determining your values, it's time to envision the life you desire. Consider the following questions:

- How is your day structured?
- Where do you live?
- What values do you hold?
- How do you use your free time?

Clarify your vision

Clearly define your goals. What kind of career, relationships and lifestyle do you desire? Spend some time reflecting on your dreams and aspirations. Describe your vision to move closer to your objectives, as it will act as a road map.

Set objectives

Now you've identified your values; it's time to set your goals. What action points will you put in place to achieve your dream life?

_____
_____
_____
_____
_____

She is Limitless

_____
_____
_____

> **Make a plan for your goals by breaking them into manageable steps.**

Take action
While having goals is essential, taking action is necessary to make them meaningful. Making an effort to seek a mentor and upgrading your skills will help you to reach your goals faster.

Be open to change
The life you desire involves change since it's continuously evolving. Even though change is unsettling, we should accept it but not remain complacent. Remember that every step you take towards your dream is a step away from your desired life.

Maintaining your flexibility
Due to life's unpredictability, our plans occasionally turn out differently than we intended. For this reason, we must learn how to remain flexible and willing to adjust plans as and when required. Remember that progress, not perfection is what matters.

She is Limitless

Surround yourself with positive people
This is my all-time favourite – speak with trusted friends, family, networking groups and mentors who are able to provide advice and direction. Avoid being around negativity and concentrate on what motivates and encourages you.

Don't allow your circumstances to limit your potential. Don't settle for a mediocre life when you have the power to create an extraordinary life.

Your life is a journey, not a destination and requires constant reflection, ongoing effort and taking action. You can achieve your dreams with perseverance, dedication, passion, and hard work. You can create a life that's truly your own by implementing the tips mentioned in this book.

Start today by making gradual steps because the opportunities are limitless!

She is Limitless

---- Epilogue ----
~

"When the world says: "Give up", hope whispers: "Try one more time."

Author Unknown.

My life is a reflection of the above quote and serves as a daily reminder to keep pushing. Each day represents fresh opportunities to chase after my dreams. The world's challenges may tempt us to give up due to failures and setbacks. However, determine to keep it moving. In the words of Michael Chang, **"If at first, you don't succeed, try again!"**

Looking back, I realise my parents gave me a precious gift; the notion that anything is possible! They gave me self-assurance and fortitude through the most trying situations. For this reason, I promised to create a legacy for future generations. Just like my parents did for me, I speak encouraging and empowering words to my children and loved ones. I am here today because of what I did in the past, and I continue to press on with my head high and my heart full of HOPE!

Although we face unique challenges and our dreams may look different to what we originally envisioned, it doesn't

She is Limitless

make them less valuable. Special mothers ought to be free to pursue their goals rather than being constrained by the parameters of their current identity. With proper guidance and assistance, anything is possible!

Special mothers are capable of achieving anything and shouldn't allow anyone to tell them otherwise.

Mothers with children who have exceptional needs should constantly strive to lead joyful and fulfilling lives. As a result, they'll support their children more effectively and assist them in reaching their full potential. Special mothers must focus on the future and work towards their objectives for their families and themselves. They should utilise the tools and support systems available to them. Special needs mothers will benefit significantly from these resources, whether financial support, career counselling or therapy.

Making time for yourself is crucial for preserving your physical and mental well-being and improving your ability to be present and involved with the family. We are all here for a reason. The secret to achieving your personal goals and finding pleasure is persistence, the drive to act, and the ability to request and accept assistance when required. We must develop patience and devotion during our motherhood journey to stay sane and give our loved

She is Limitless

ones the finest care possible. Yet, amidst the daily struggles of emotional ups and downs, don't forget the Power of Hope.

Remember that HOPE isn't just a feeling. As you go on this journey, HOPE is the vital lifeline and motivating force that will see you through the testing moments, giving you a sense of direction. Whilst HOPE may not solve all our problems, it gives us the strength to face each day head-on despite the obstacles and setbacks.

I urge all mothers and caregivers to embrace the power of HOPE and POSSIBILITY and let them inspire you to achieve the impossible. Never give up on your aspirations. Instead, dare to dream big and accomplish your goals by having confidence in yourself, setting objectives, taking action and being consistent. Finally, realise your purpose for being here, which is to make a difference in the world.

Remember that anything you put your mind to will become a reality. As easy as it may be, avoid feeling pressured to live up to society's expectations as a mother of a child with special needs. Don't let your circumstances dictate your future; instead, transform your pain into purpose. We have what it takes to dream and accomplish all possibilities for ourselves and our families by embracing our strengths and putting in the necessary effort to achieve our goals.

She is Limitless

---- Useful books which helped me on My Journey with Twin Angels ----

Seven Habits of Highly Successful People – Stephen R. Covey
Stephen R. Covey explained in his book that to be successful in every aspect of life, I had to change my perception of the world to understand and define what success means to me.

Eat That Frog – Brian Tracy
By urging us to master time management skills and tackle the most challenging jobs first, Brian Tracy offers 21 suggestions in Eat that Frog to help you stop procrastinating and do more in less time. You can get fantastic outcomes, success and a feeling of personal power and fulfilment by putting them into practice until they become a natural part of you. The key is to start taking action immediately.

Think And Grow Rich – Napoleon Hill
To put it in simple terms, our thoughts are powerful, and you become anything your mind imagines being possible. As a result, your mind becomes the only tool that has the potential to stop you from becoming the best version of yourself or drive you in that direction.

She is Limitless

Becoming – Michelle Obama
Becoming is a must-read for working mothers who want it all, especially understanding the journey to self-discovery and life's purpose. She emphasises in her book that when we are aligned with our purpose, leaping into the unknown isn't going to harm us, and we will be far from poor. On the contrary, it will follow us when we pursue our purpose. For this reason, we should prioritise our happiness, and everything else will fall into place. Skin colour is irrelevant. It makes no difference to what accent you have. Age is irrelevant. All that matters is who we can help and how we can make a difference in the world. We may accomplish this by discovering our life's purpose and living it daily.

The Light We Carry – Michelle Obama
In The Light We Carry, the former First Lady shares practical wisdom and powerful strategies for staying hopeful and balanced in today's uncertain world. A mother, daughter, spouse and friend, she shares new stories, insightful reflections on change, and the wisdom that helps her become who she is. With her trademark humour, honesty, and compassion, Michelle explores issues connected to race, gender, and visibility, encouraging readers to work through their fears, find strength in the community, and live with boldness. The Light We Carry inspired me to examine my life, identify

sources of joy and connect meaningfully to others in a turbulent world.

The Richest Man in Babylon – George S. Clason
The Richest Man in Babylon reminds me not to waste good opportunities and always trust my instincts. Keep track of expenses and invest wisely. Find measures to protect yourself from losses and prepare for retirement. Earn while you can, but always plan for the future.

The Gifts of Imperfection: let go of who you think you're supposed to be and embrace who you are – Brene Brown
The Gift of Imperfection teaches me to embrace and accept myself without fear of judgement.

You Are Badass: How to stop doubting your greatness and start living an awesome life – Jen Sincero
You Are a Badass helped me to confront and change self-sabotaging behaviours and create a life filled with meaning and purpose. My takeaway lessons from the book are as follows:

- What you choose to focus on becomes your reality
- Your faith should be greater than your fears
- Actions reveal answers better than sitting and thinking about them

She is Limitless

- If you want to make changes in your life and get what you want, you have to take control over your thoughts
- Living in a state of gratitude helps you believe that something greater is coming your way
- When we tell ourselves we are unqualified for something, we express fear; not that we can't do it.

This book is an excellent reminder of our abilities which shape our lives. If you have self-doubt, limiting beliefs, feel stuck or can't see yourself in a place of success, wealth, happiness or thriving in whatever you want to do, this book informs you of how to change and do better.

Good Vibes, Good Life: How self-love is the key to unlocking your greatness – Vex King

In his book, Vex King challenged me to be more mindful, practise self-care, overcome toxic energy, put my well-being first, cultivate positive lifestyle habits, and change my beliefs to experience greater opportunities. I am continuously discovering my purpose to become a shining beacon for others to manifest my goals through tried-and-tested methods.

You can find all the above books on Amazon.

She is Limitless

---- What's Next? ----

Whether you're a special needs mother or someone who is frustrated and overwhelmed with various aspects of life, as you turn the final pages of this book and take control over your life, continue on the path to finding empowerment and fulfilment by maintaining an optimistic attitude despite life's ups and downs and never give up on your aspirations.

Join our Facebook Community
Are you tired of feeling isolated in raising a child with special needs? Are you looking for a community of like-minded mothers where you can connect with those facing similar challenges? Look no further than our Facebook group *(mumrevamped)* where special mothers truly get it. Our group is a safe and welcoming space where we support, inspire, and celebrate one another. You can share experiences, ask for advice and find comfort in the company of mothers who understand.

Together, we can support, create a powerful network and help our children thrive. We discuss self-care, wellness, stress management and, most importantly, building a solid, resilient mindset enabling us to go after our dreams fearlessly and without guilt. You will receive further details once you subscribe to my email list on www.mumrevamped.co.uk. Once you click on the

She is Limitless

website, scroll down and enter your email address in the 'Sign up" section.

Online courses
Our courses empower you to be unstoppable; you will learn various subjects including self-care practises, journaling, and creating vision boards. Find out more information on: www.mumrevamped.co.uk.

Help me spread my message
If you enjoyed reading **She is Limitless**, I'd appreciate a book review on Goodreads, Amazon, and my website on: www.mumrevamped.co.uk

Helping to spread my message will start conversations about: "Who cares for the Caregiver?"

---- References ----

Chapter 1
Hollywood Foundation: https://hollyrod.org/our-mission/

Understanding the 5 stages of grief: https://www.cruse.org.uk/understanding-grief/effects-of-grief/five-stages-of-grief/

Chapter 3
Dear Mom of a Child with a Disability, I Celebrate You: https://www.ellenstumbo.com/dear-special-needs-mama-i-celebrate-you/

Chapter 4
Yolanda Adams (Never Give Up) Lyrics: https://www.azlyrics.com/lyrics/yolandaadams/nevergiveup.html

Chapter 8
Medsafe: The Nocebo Effect: https://medsafe.govt.nz/profs/PUArticles/March2019/The%20nocebo%20effect.htm

The Nocebo Effect: https://drdavidhamilton.com/the-nocebo-effect/

The Power of The Placebo Effect:
https://www.health.harvard.edu/mental-health/the-power-of-the-placebo-effect

The Power of Your Mind: Placebo and Nocebo Effect:
https://sanguinebio.com/2020/07/22/the-power-of-your-mind-placebo-and-nocebo-effects/

What is the Placebo Effect?
https://www.webmd.com/pain-management/what-is-the-placebo-effect

Chapter 13
Parade: 100 Quotes About Self-Care, Because Being Good to Yourself Has Never Been More Important:
https://parade.com/1070248/maureenmackey/self-care-quotes/

Parenting ADHD and Autism:
https://parentingadhdandautism.com/2014/07/momma-self-care/

Planned Parenthood – Six Types of Self-Care:
https://secure.everyaction.com/p/Pg5bqblugE6-NGId09RIcQ2

Put Your Oxygen Mask on First:
https://www.donnaschilder.com/articles/life-coaching-articles/put-your-oxygen-mask-on-first/

Taking Care of YOU: Self-Care for Family Caregivers:
https://www.caregiver.org/resource/taking-care-you-self-care-family-caregivers/

The Critical Need for Self-Care: The Oxygen Mask Rule:
https://www.autismparentingmagazine.com/self-care-oxygen-mask-rule/

Chapter 14
Philadelphia College of Osteopathic Medicine (Noelle Cauda-Laufer, 2017):
https://digitalcommons.pcom.edu/cgi/viewcontent.cgi?article=1434&context=psychology_dissertations

www.ingramcontent.com/pod-product-compliance
Lightning Source LLC
Chambersburg PA
CBHW081229080526
44587CB00022B/3871